The Immortal
VICTOR TRUMPER

By the Same Author

CRICKET CRISIS

BRIGHTLY FADES THE DON

THE ASHES CROWN THE YEAR

MASTERS OF CRICKET

BROWN AND COMPANY: THE TOUR IN AUSTRALIA

THE GREATEST TEST OF ALL

FINGLETON ON CRICKET

The Immortal
VICTOR TRUMPER

J. H. FINGLETON

Foreword by
W. J. (Bill) O'Reilly

COLLINS
London and Sydney
1978

William Collins Sons & Co. Ltd.
London · Glasgow · Sydney · Auckland
Toronto · Johannesburg

First published 1978
© J. H. Fingleton 1978

ISBN 0 00 216807 3

Set in Lino Pilgrim
Made and Printed in Great Britain by
William Collins Sons & Co. Ltd. Glasgow

To
Sir Robert Menzies, a long-time friend and ardent
cricket enthusiast

Contents

Foreword		9
Acknowledgements		13
Author's Note		17
1	'God Bless Victor Trumper'	21
2	Paddington	42
3	Early Days	51
4	A Fluke Trip to England	61
5	The First English Tour	68
6	How Trumper Skinned Redfern	83
7	Trumper's Technique	94
8	Two Fine Innings	113
9	The Commerce of Cricket	125
10	Trumper against the Googly	138
11	The 'Big Six' Upheaval	142
12	Trumper's Benefit	153
13	The Last Great Innings	159
14	Death of a Cricketer	165
Chronology		172
Trumper's Record		174
Bradman's Record		194
Index		203

Illustration Credits

Foreword

by Bill O'Reilly

The responsibility, the duty, the privilege and the pleasure of feeding back to cricket lovers the fascinating stories of a beloved and legendary hero – I write of course of Victor Trumper – have in the past all been side-stepped. Cricket biographers have thought it fitter to proliferate on subjects of much lesser account, or else have found it more comfortable to take the easy way out—to dodge a job that bristled with difficulties and produce instead a quick pot-boiler.

The true value of the present magnificent book – ninth on the Jack Fingleton literary production line – will be assessed from the reactions it arouses in our cricketing memory-bank. No cricket writer has ever had a more inspiring subject upon which to work, nor has there been a more exacting effort required to handle it efficiently. For Fingleton's research, you will quickly become aware, has been a stupendous task. Not only has he collected his information from every possible source in all cricket countries, but he has substantiated every bit of it before presenting it in its niche in cricket history.

As people well know, many fine tales are told with bated breath of old-time performers – Doctor Grace, for instance – which score appreciative applause at cricket dinners where entertainment value rates very much higher than authenticity. This has been one of the more difficult areas confronting Fingleton.

Take, if you will, the wide-spread story of Don Bradman's solitary entry in his bowling analyses in Anglo-Australian Tests. Browsing through those impressive records of his you will find hidden among mountainous batting figures the intriguing fact that he managed to snare only one reluctant Englishman with his seldom-publicized bowling techniques. Turn to the relevant match and then, the next time you join in one of those free-for-all 'I remember' sessions, which all cricketers love just as dearly as the Irish do a wake, start the ball rolling by saying,

'I remember Bradman bowling Walter Hammond with a full toss in Adelaide in 1933.' Then sit back for the next half-hour, listening to the arguments that follow.

All the relevant facts stated above are perfectly true. Yet at the end of the first half-hour of your free-for-all you may well count yourself lucky if the site, Adelaide, has been established and accepted. It's well worth a trial if you wish to find out how wide-ranging is the tide of imagination when a little bit of hero-worship is brought to play.

The story itself has all the ingredients required for a saga. Woodfull, a very careful captain who took even less tactical risks than did Bradman himself, handed the ball to his batting maestro crossing all his fingers – that is, of course, the ones still sufficiently supple in that bodyline year. Hammond had reached 85 in a characteristically aggressive late-afternoon workout that had the Australian attack, as I knew very well, literally down on all its fours.

Bradman delivered a king-size slow full-toss which, had it ever hit the ground, would have commenced to go slowly through its intended leg-break routine, at some point situated indefinitely between the 'keeper, Vic Richardson, who was deputizing for the injured Oldfield, and wide short slip, Stan McCabe. Hammond, reasonably enough, decided to demolish the members' stand with a massive square-cut. Sure enough, he connected – only for the ball to cannon back from bat to stumps. Hammond b. Bradman 85. I narrate this true version of the facts to give you an opportunity to imagine for yourself what troubles faced Jack Fingleton when he sat down to this demanding assignment.

It would be fair, I suppose, in making the statement I did about Bradman's capacity to say that, very occasionally, he did accept some risks in doing this job which places him high among the great Australian captains. In Melbourne in 1937, for instance, he ordered me to the wicket, ineffectual bat in hand, to open Australia's second innings. The grave risk he took then was that I might have laid such heavy claim to tenure of the lofty position that Jack Fingleton's claims to it were gone forever. As it turned out, it took no more than a few fleeting seconds for Bill Voce to resolve that matter to Fingleton's advantage. Next day, however, I noticed that Fingleton showed such extraordinary concern over the threat that he tore off a magnificent century to help open Australia's highly successful counter-attack in that see-sawing series. I have never let him forget that his career walked on a tight-rope that dismal first afternoon!

On another yet similar tack, I myself have cause to believe that the time-honoured cricket arena known to us all as the Oval must have the capacity to expand itself like the famous frog about which old Aesop wrote. If all the Englishmen who have said on being introduced to me in any place I've visited around the world since 1938, 'O'Reilly, yes, how nice! I have very fond memories of you bowling to Len Hutton at the Oval when he topped Don Bradman's record Test score' were *really* eye-witnesses Wembley itself would have been 'busted', as I was. Len must have brought down all Yorkshire and whomever he could muster from Lancashire for the historic occasion. I had no idea free tickets were so plentiful then.

I first became a team-mate of Jack Fingleton the best part of fifty years ago, and I put him to the test many times as he stood close at short-leg – or 'silly leg' as we advisedly referred to it – while I got on with the job of practising length and direction. I was also with him in the Australia and New South Wales sides when he transcended the very heights of cricket heroism as he withstood the bodyline onslaught of the 1932/3 series. In fact, it would be safe to say the Fingletons and the O'Reillys have been teaming together right from the time of Brian Boru or, better still, since St Patrick himself taught them all to say their prayers.

Yet Jack Fingleton is at risk in asking me to carry out this ceremonial task of holding his precious baby in my arms at its baptismal font. I'm out of practice for such responsibility. I note, with shaking knees, that Sir Neville Cardus, Sir Norman Birkett and Sir Robert Menzies have all performed nobly when they joined Fingleton's team at differing times since he started his pen flowing with *Cricket Crisis* back in 1946.

There is only one way in which I could successfully have been per-suaded to take issue with one, or all three of them, if you like, and that would have been with a six-stitcher, with seam slightly raised, in my right hand. Certainly not with this pen. By comparison with them I feel like Sir Robert did when he reminisced with his accustomed mastery at a London dinner in 1953. Speaking to a receptive audience at a function he had himself arranged, he did honour to Mr Hector Morrison, then Speaker of the House of Commons, later to become a grievously short-lived Governor-General of Australia as Lord Dunrossil.

Warming to his pleasant task of assuring a mainly-English guest-list that he was deeply appreciative of the respect Englishmen, in general,

had for him, he stared, it seemed, straight down the table on his right
wing where I sat surrounded by ex-English cricket captains. If it were
support he was seeking it was certainly not forthcoming from me, who
had struggled throughout the session with Douglas Jardine, Gubby Allen
and Freddie Brown to maintain some feeble Australian equilibrium.

Our great Prime Minister went on to say: 'Englishmen, generally,
I think, take a more sympathetic view towards me than do my fellow
Australians. Indeed, there are some Australians who take the advantage
of referring to me as "Pig Iron Bob".'

Lowering his mellifluous voice as though to save the feelings of the
magnificently-clad Master of Ceremonies, who stood to the rear, Sir
Robert went on: 'There are many of my countrymen, I would have you
know, who would swear that I am the greatest bastard ever to set foot
in their country.'

He got no further. Reacting to a vigorous nudge in the left-hand ribs,
I turned defensively to a seemingly highly-resentful Jardine, with his
Scottish blood mounting to the challenge of yet another Pretender.
'Bill,' he said, 'the learned gentleman is miserably misinformed. He
could not possibly be listed higher than number two . . . and well I know
it.' I took his point, and for the first time during the evening readily
admitted the strength of his implied argument.

By comparison with those three heavyweights aforementioned, I submit yet again.

I would have loved to have written this book. Nothing in my cricket
career could possibly have pleased me more. Having watched it grow and
now having finally devoured it, I have a better understanding of what
General John Wolfe meant in comparing his scaling of the heights of
Abraham with Gray's writing of his elegy.

Consequently, I take enormous pleasure and team-sharing pride from
the satisfying knowledge that all the cheering and applause for this great
performance goes to Jack Fingleton for an historic job that has cried out
so loudly and so long for attention.

Acknowledgements

So many people have helped me over this book that any brief note of acknowledgement is impossible. After I had sent a letter to the Editor of the *Sydney Morning Herald*, Guy Harriot, asking for information about Trumper's career, I was astounded at the number of letters I received, proof that Trumper is still not only remembered but continues to be a legend in NSW and Australian cricket. It was to be evidence, too, of how many people were to make contributions to the finished book, and I therefore thought it best to include a Trumper 'Scroll of Honour', and I do so with thanks to the following:

Victor Trumper junior, *Chatswood, NSW*. Mrs Syd Trumper, *Lindfield, NSW*. Sir Charles Victor Smith, *Canberra*. Bill Mandle, *Australian National University*, W. A. D. Glossop, *Totley Rise, Sheffield, England*. Sid Harper, *Ealing, London, W5*. Belinda Gemmell (my daughter), *Killara, NSW*. Jacquelyn Fingleton (my daughter), *Roseville, NSW*. Malcolm Gemmell, *Killara, NSW*. Dick Brittenden, *Christchurch, New Zealand*. Walter Hadlee, *Christchurch, New Zealand*. Dr Bob Mitchell, *Canberra*. Dr Larry Fingleton (my son), *Roseville, NSW*. Bob Radford (*Secretary, NSWCA*), *Sydney, NSW*. Allison Altham, *Winchester, Hampshire, England*. Louise Percy, *Canberra*. Peter Hardacre, *Canberra*. Graham Howard, *Canberra*. Ross Middleton, *Melbourne, Victoria*. Dick Coombs, *Canberra*. Tom Veivers (*Secretary, QCA*), *Brisbane*. Bede Nairn, *Australian National University*. Prof. Paddy Moran, *Australian National University*. Prof. Finn Crisp, *Australian National University*. Bill Pederson, *Canberra*. C. E. ('Nip') Pellew, *Walkersville, South Australia*. Leigh Winser, *Barwon Heads, Victoria*. Jack Lonsdale, *Librarian, Times Newspapers, London*. Ramsey Milne, *Johannesburg*. Charles Barry, *Johannesburg*. Most Rev. Sir Marcus Loane, *Anglican Archbishop of Sydney*. Alan McGilvray, *ABC, Sydney*. Gwen McGilvray, *Double Bay, NSW*. Tal Duckmanton, *ABC, Sydney*. Ray Robinson, *Northbridge, NSW*. Brendan Belson, *Canberra*. Keith Traynor, *Red Hill, Canberra*. Keith Butler, *Adelaide*

Advertiser, *South Australia*. Dom Martin Salmon, *Downside, Stratton-on-the-fosse, England*. Barbara Isaacs, *Shepton Mallett, Somerset, England*. Ruth Massie, *Worcestershire, England*. Mike Massie, *Worcestershire, England*. Ruth Kippax, *Street, Somerset, England*. Adrian Donaldson, *Blaxland, NSW*. Bruce Donaldson, *Blaxland, NSW*. Guy Harriott, SMH, *Sydney*. J. P. Wood, *Secretary*, (*SCG*), *Sydney*. John Luff, *Litton, Somerset*. Edith Luff, *Litton, Somerset*. Irvine Rosenwater, *London*. Gladys Grieve, *Lane Cove, NSW*. Don Chipp, MHR, *Hotham, Victoria*. Grey Fingleton (my son), *Randwick, NSW*. Sean McGrath, *Dublin*. Mrs N. G. Addison, *Bundanoon, NSW*. Albert Bridges, *St. Mary's, NSW*. Brian Monfries, *Port Macquarie, NSW*. Gilbert Mant, *Port Macquarie, NSW*. R. T. Johnson, *Elizabeth Bay, NSW*. Mick Alterator, *Waverley, NSW*. Wendy Wimbush, *Muswell Hill, London*. H. T. Fry, *Killarney Vale, Gosford, NSW*. Philip K. Rpappein, *Collaroy, NSW*. Brendan Kelson, *Canberra, ACT*. Willy Blum, *Aranda, ACT*. Lillian Dunn, *North Sydney, NSW*. Mrs Fay Chisholm, *Rotorua, New Zealand*. Staff, Mitchell and Public Library, *Sydney*. Staff, Australian National Library, *Canberra*. V. McDonnell, *Punchbowl, NSW*. Reg Fusedale, *Kogarah, NSW*. The Right Hon. Sir William McKell, *Double Bay*. Harry Wittenburg, *Bellvue Hill, NSW*. R. V. Pockley, *Double Bay, NSW*. Les R. Hill, *Mt. Gambier, South Australia*. Essie Mitchell, *Roseville, NSW*. M. J. Rilt, *North Sydney, NSW*. Jack F. Byrnes, *Waverley Council, NSW*. John Hook, *Paddington, NSW*. Gordon Mallet, *Beacon Hill, NSW*. A. Coningsby, *Melbourne South, Victoria*. Tom Ferrier, *Lane Cove, NSW*. Jim Meehan, President S. Melb. CC, *Melbourne, Victoria*. S. Green, Curator, Museum, *Lord's, London. NW8*. Jack Deeth, Cumberland CC, *Parramatta, NSW*. J. McAtamney, *Kogarah, NSW*. E. W. Adams, *Kogarah, NSW*. Allan C. Dempster, *Wavell's Heights, Brisbane*. Isabella A. Atkinson, *Collaroy Plateau, NSW*. Lynn Fuller, *North Glenelg, South Australia*. Clarrie Grimmett, *Adelaide, South Australia*. Len Darling, *Adelaide, South Australia*.

To a number of people, also, I owe a special note of thanks. My mentor for this book, for instance, has been Eric McElhone, an octogenarian Sydney solicitor, who played under Trumper's captaincy for NSW and who often played against him for the North Sydney Club. He knew him well, collected articles on him, and has given many Trumper lectures. He has provided me with much material, and has urged me constantly, over a considerable period, to write this biography. I am indebted, too, to Cedric Emanuel, the outstanding Australian artist, for the drawing of Trumper's old home, and I also received much help from the Australian National University. George Franki, of the University of NSW, another tremendous cricket enthusiast, was of incalculable assistance and encouragement. Jim Coldham compiled the meticulous Index. Tom Trumble, trustee of the Melbourne Cricket Ground and son of the famed Hugh, who played so often with Trumper, was a great help, as was D. K. Darling, son of Joe, the Australian captain, who lent me pictures of his father from his own book, *Test Tussles*. Bill Mandle was most generous in giving me permission to use his material on the early days of cricketers in England and Australia, and I am, finally, greatly indebted to my old friend and playing comrade Bill O'Reilly, for so generously agreeing to give of his time away from the fish and writing me his splendid Foreword.

Author's Note

It amazes me that no book was ever written on Victor Trumper during his lifetime, when rich material was available and at a time which abounded with splendid writers on the game. It is more than difficult to attempt the task (for instance, he kept no diary, and very few letters survive), yet I feel this book may help to do something to honour and perpetuate his name.

Why such a note of piety over someone who, after all, was 'only' a cricketer? Daniel Reese reflects my own feelings in his book *Was it all Cricket?* when he says that there was a charm about Trumper that won a warm spot in the hearts of all who knew him. He goes on:

> He was one of the most modest and unselfish of players. He accepted umpires' decisions as a matter of course, and no one ever heard him say there was a doubt about a decision when he came back in the pavilion. Australians and Englishmen alike honour the memory of Trumper. He left behind him a record and a reputation that shine like a planet in the history of the game.

There was never any suggestion of side or swank about him. He spoke seldom and then in a quiet, restrained voice. He was never noisy or ebullient and was always doing things for his fellows; in fact he was the perfect team-mate and travelling companion, taking burdens on his shoulders that others avoided. For example, other members of an Australian eleven were known to avoid the welcoming committees on railway stations and would dash off down side-streets to get to their hotel first to seek a good or a single room; but Trumper was always ready to take what came his way and to be just an ordinary team member.

In fact he shunned publicity and crowds as much as he could, and was plainly embarrassed when he returned to the plaudits of the pavilion.

It is said that when he travelled to the city from his home in Chatswood he would catch the train to McMahon's Point and then go up the front of the ferry across the harbour because he feared he would be recognized and drawn by some enthusiast into a talk on cricket. Likewise, he could not stand the bragger. The story is told of a Waverley player who had previously played with Paddington and said he knew how to get Trumper out. The player was Tommy Rose, who could bowl both with right and left hand, and often did. Tommy made the mistake of confiding what he thought to his team-mates. The 'boast' got to Trumper's ears, and he was waiting for Rose when he came on to bowl in the second innings. As Noble, Trumper's skipper, said: 'Everybody was agog when this young spinner came on to bowl against Victor.' As Rose bowled the first ball Trumper went down the pitch after it, hit it long and low and it bounced over the fence for four. The next hit the fence on the full. The following four balls were hit out of the ground (Hampden Oval, since re-named 'Trumper Park') for six. The first and second balls of the young bowler's next over were played quietly by Trumper's partner Charlie Winning, who scored a single off the second. Trumper played the third ball without scoring and then hit the next three for six. Thus he received ten balls and scored 50 runs off nine of them in five and a quarter minutes. Needless to say, the young bowler was taken off, a sadder and wiser man. There was a capacity crowd, for thousands followed Trumper in those days whenever he played in Sydney, and in the midst of the excitement the boundary fence of pickets between the pavilion and the ground collapsed in the general excitement. No more was said of how to get Trumper back in the pavilion.

A one-time team-mate, Frank Iredale, in his book *33 Years of Cricket* thought it was futile to try to depict Victor Trumper the man. Nevertheless he tried:

To be near him seemed to me to be an honour. His was one of those natures which called you to and in whose presence you felt it good to live. His loving nature made many friends. I never knew anybody who practised self-effacement as much as he did. He loved cricket and respected those who played it. In victory or defeat he was the same – his demeanour never changed. If by any chance a player coveted a bat he used he gave it to him. At times it became embarrassing for his many friends to avoid his favours. I never knew a cricketer who showed his emotions so little. One could not read his mind, therefore he was not understood. Everything he did was taken for granted. It was never necessary to ask him to do anything in a match because he knew what was going to be asked. No work was too hard for him and if he did more than his share no word passed his lips.

If there was a bad seat in a train, he was in it. If the sleeping compartment happened to be over the wheels, one could always be sure that Victor would change his place to take it. On the steamer going to England he was always helping somebody. If the steward offered an apology for the food, he would say, 'It really doesn't matter. I am not a bit hungry.' . . . His nature was just as hard to describe as his cricket, because one cannot recall in one's acquaintance with men a nature like his.

He was splendidly loyal, and a firm and just believer in what was right. He was a hard man to know, because he made you so indebted to him for many kindnesses. Children loved him because he was so easily approachable and so adaptable. He thought of others so constantly that one could almost believe he lived for the rest of the world.

That gives a good insight into Trumper's remarkable character, one all the more remarkable when one learns that he was brought up in a suburb of Sydney, parts of which were rightly regarded as slum areas. Paddington, as the suburb was called, together with its neighbour, Darlinghurst, were the haunts of larrikins, who used to indulge in gang warfare, smashing windows and using the piles of blue metal round about as weapons in street fights. The denizens of Paddington were known as the cockneys of Sydney – quick with a quid and a quip. So it was all the more odd that Trumper, living in this atmosphere at a time when the original 'Ockers' were to obtrude themselves into Australian life, should have been such a perfect tourist and gentleman.

Cricket can so often be the most selfish of games – as it is played sometimes, anyway; but no one has a word to say against Trumper's behaviour, his thoughts for other players, or the way he lived, on or off the field. Nobody knows better the character and manliness of a cricketer than his team-mates, who live, travel and tour with him and see the same face each morning at breakfast. It is easy to become intolerant of a man and his mannerisms during a long tour. But among his fellows it was 'Vic this' or 'Vic that' when they spoke of him, which they did with reverence and a far-away look in their eyes. No cricketer, surely, has known such love and abject affection from his fellow men. This book has sprung out of that love.

1

'God Bless Victor Trumper'

Victor Trumper revolutionized batting. Others had better figures or higher averages, but figures seldom tell the true story. It was what Trumper achieved and how he did it that made him stand out from his fellows. He prospered, too, in a golden age, an era which saw the great Ranjitsinhji, Fry, MacLaren, Spooner *et al*, and which had just known the immortal Dr W. G. Grace and was soon to know John Berry Hobbs.

For me, Trumper remains the greatest batsman who ever lived. Bradman could rightly be advanced against him, but whereas Bradman, in the early stages of his career, operated upon bowlers like a butcher at the abattoirs, wading deep in their agony and frustration, Trumper was like a surgeon, deftly and classically dissecting everything that was offered against him.

I realize that this is a large claim to make for Trumper, and later in this book I argue in detail why for me he possessed all the gifts, and how it is still possible to appreciate his skills. One of the problems, of course, of getting a modern audience to appreciate Trumper is that here is someone who was at his peak at the turn of the century, more than seventy years ago: is it really possible to bring his achievements to life? I believe it is, but in this chapter am going to let his contemporaries speak for themselves.

The man who wrote most interestingly about Trumper was Colonel Philip Trevor, CBE, in his book *Cricket and Cricketers*. He regrets he did not see Trumper in England in 1899, his first tour, or in 1902, when Darling's team came over and Trumper enjoyed a great year, but when the Colonel himself was still in South Africa. He did not get a real chance to study the Australian champion till 1905 – not a good season for Trumper – but he saw plenty of him in Australia when Trevor was manager of the 1907–8 English team. He writes:

For all practical purposes we may take it that Trumper's real career was limited to a space of ten to a dozen years. Cricket – let us always bear in mind – is not a thing apart and the analogies of greater life are applicable to the cricket field. Did not the younger Pitt, Byron, Napoleon, Hannibal, Frederick the Great, Mascagni, Kipling, to quote only a few of the best-known names, sit in the seats of the mighty? Again, Trumper owes his reputation more to how he did things than to the things he did. He only got half a dozen centuries in Test matches, and, indeed, if the arithmetical test is the only one by which a batsman is to be tried, there are a good many claimants for the place which Trumper, in the considered opinion of many of the experts, holds.

It may seem a strange statement to make, and yet I will say that in some respects the subtlety of Trumper's strokes was even more concealed than it was in the strokes which Ranji made. However closely you watched Trumper, it was inordinately difficult to follow exactly what he was doing with his bat. Trumper, we know, could hit the ball 'half way round the clock'. I will try to substantiate that statement at the risk of being prosaic. Extend the bowling-crease (the one, of course, at Trumper's back) to the boundary on both sides of the ground; then bowl to Trumper an ordinary, medium-paced, good-length ball. Trumper could hit that ball to any spot on the boundary in front of that extended white line. That is a feat in itself – a feat which even Ranji might be put to it to accomplish. And that is not all. Suppose Trumper hit every ball of that over in the following order: the first to point (square), the second through the covers, the third evading mid-off, the fourth more or less straight, the fifth to mid-on, and the sixth to square-leg. You would watch these successful strokes, and you could not tell accurately as the bat came on to the ball the exact direction in which the batsman intended the ball to go. Trumper knew it himself almost to the 'minute of a degree'. His knowledge, indeed, of batting angles was too exact for the ordinary eye to follow. I am still blessed with good distance eyesight. I can read figures and names on hoardings in a way that ought to make advertisers feel that they have not spent their money in vain. The bull's eye at Bisley 1000 yards away is to me a clear and finished piece of work, though the sights of my rifle would now have to be adjusted with the aid of field-glasses.

But I was made to stop swaggering about my long-distance sight when Trumper put his bat on the ball. I used to find myself guessing and I nearly always guessed wrong. I predicted a square-cut as the ball flashed through the air, and then the ball would go in front of cover-point. I was worse fogged by the strokes to the 'on' and hopelessly baffled with the square-leg hits. Good-length bowling just meant nothing to Trumper.

When I say I did not see him at his very best, I mean that I did not see him for a considerable period of the time during which he remained at his very best. But of course I have seen him play many an innings in which his comrades admitted him to be at his best. It was on these occasions that he dealt with the good-length balls in the way that an ordinary forcing first-class batsman deals with half-volleys and long hops. Our steadiest professional bowlers, indeed, have said that they would rather bowl to Ranji than bowl to Trumper. They knew, they said, more exactly the extent of evil that could happen to them when they bowled to him than when they bowled to Trumper.

Of all disheartening balls which they could bowl, the straight, good-length one was, from their point of view, the most disheartening of all. It was sent either past point or to the square-leg boundary – even over the square-leg boundary – according to Trumper's mood at the moment of making the stroke. As I watched, I got desperately anxious to analyse the inner workings of the batsman's mind, or the thing it was that was causing the man's mood. That he was fearless, physically and morally, a schoolboy could not fail to know, and that he must have been self-confident goes without saying. Yet if there is such a thing as modesty in a successful public performer, man or woman, Victor Trumper was modest. He was very kind-hearted; he was very generous, and generous in thought as well as deed. If he was not simple he was the greatest actor who ever lived, and personally I do not think he was an actor at all. Trumper was certainly a peculiar blend. In his batting strokes you seemed to recognize all the athletic simplicity of W.G. with most of the subtlety of Ranji. Certainly Trumper was athlete and artist, though I believe the majority of spectators were more convinced of his athleticism than of his art. He was a perfect timer of the ball; yet as he played some of his strokes I could not tell whether it was forearm or wrist which he was using the more.

You always knew when Ranji was using his wrists, but one wondered if in the making of some of his most marvellous strokes Trumper himself was aware whether chief marks should go to shoulders, forearms or wrists. It was a case, indeed, of blend, and blend was the essence of Trumper's batting.

What I have tried to say may, perhaps, help some people to understand what manner of man Trumper was, and, more or less consequently, why his batting was what it was. But he remains a baffling personality for all that.

He was not gauche; but he was shy. He loved cricket, and he enjoyed himself hugely, though without vainglory, when he was batting. But he did not love what have been called the attendant glories of the cricket field. The enthusiastic cheering of the crowd did not encourage him. On the other hand, the absence of that sort of thing did not put him off. Once in Australia I actually saw – or, should I say, heard? – Trumper barracked. I resist the temptation to moralize on the transient value of a cricket crowd's attitude to a popular hero. It made no difference to Trumper at all. He just smiled good-naturedly.

That is about the best analysis I have read of Trumper on the cricket field. Now let us see him off the field, again through the eyes of Frank Iredale, so often a team-mate of Trumper's, who wrote feelingly of him both as a cricketer and as a man. Iredale noted how difficult it was to do Trumper credit, and mentions in particular a time in the Manchester Test in 1899 when they were both in the outfield, waiting for a new batsman to come in. On such occasions, far from home – and the same applies when MCC are in Australia – players love to yarn about what is going on and how they see things. 'Trumper was loving his first trip to England,' wrote Iredale,

and the experiences he was going through, but I felt, somehow or other, his mind and thoughts were of home; he loved his home and the ties that surrounded it and though he came with us on many occasions to theatres and elsewhere, one felt that whatever may have been his thoughts of his trip, his thoughts were mainly of home.

To see him at his best, one had to go into the sanctuary of his home with his wife and his child, and there the man whom the world saw but never knew was at his best. How much he loved this life one may never know, but one felt that if all homes reflected the glory that his did it would indeed be a world worth living in. I met him on many occasions, out walking in the cool of the evening with his wife, whom he loved with a tenderness which one knew was so real, and it was on those occasions that Victor enjoyed his real pleasure in life. I came out with him and his wife from England in 1905, and it was in communion with him on this trip day after day that I got to know him so well. It was only his real friends who knew him. The cricket world knew nothing of the real man. He looked upon his cricket more as a duty than a sport. If he punished a bowler he felt sorry for him. In our old Sydney club – the Gordons –

we had many talks on the game but I never knew him to speak one word of his own part in it. He was so much apart in character from any other cricketer I knew that one almost had to confine one's talk to him of cricket in the general sense.

Arthur Mailey, one of the greatest personalities in cricket in his time, is another who has written on Trumper in his book *10 for 66 and All That*. Mailey had a rare sense of humour and was a most popular Australian in England, though he had his shortcomings as a writer on the game. For instance, he was never inclined to give much credit to O'Reilly, who early in his career wouldn't take Mailey's advice on how to grip the ball. What Mailey failed to realize was that O'Reilly had great individuality and preferred to grip the ball as he had from childhood.

Arthur, then, had his likes and dislikes in cricket; but he was a great personality and could break the ball more than anybody I knew. I played with and against him a lot during the time he played grade cricket with Balmain, and he finished his career with my old club, Waverley, under my captaincy. He could be magnificent fun, and once wrote of the team he would select to represent Australia in the first Test of a series in Australia and omitted to choose a wicket-keeper. That was typical of Arthur, who didn't worry his head much about conventions. He began life reading water meters and did a long stint with newspapers as a writer and cartoonist – in the latter being very good in drawing himself and umpires, who always wore coats that were too long and floppy white hats that came down over their ears and eyes. A splendid example of his artistic work is to be seen in the Cricketers' Club in Sydney.

Arthur finished life in the butchering business in Cronulla and, true to type, scrawled on his window : 'He bowled tripe, he wrote it, and now he's selling it.' His article on Trumper tells well what he thought when he realized he was to bowl on a certain day against his hero, Trumper. It also gives a good idea of how a ball will react to spin. Here is his article in full :

It is difficult to realize that a relatively minor event in one's life can still remain the most important through the years. I was chosen to play for Redfern against Paddington, and Paddington was Victor Trumper's club. This was unbelievable, fantastic. It could never happen – something was sure to go wrong. A war – an earthquake – Trumper might fall sick. A million things could crop up in the two or three days before the match.

I sat on my bed and looked at Trumper's picture still pinned on the canvas wall. It seemed to be breathing with the movement of the draught between the skirting. I just couldn't believe that this, to me, ethereal and godlike figure could step off the wall, pick up the bat and say: 'Two legs, please, umpire,' in my presence. My family, usually undemonstrative and self-possessed, found it difficult to maintain that reserve which, strange as it may seem, was characteristic of my father's Northern Irish heritage. 'H'm,' said Father, 'Playing against Trumper on Saturday? By Jove, you'll cop old harry if you're put on to bowl to him.' 'Why should he?' protested Mother. 'You never know what you can do until you try.'

I had nothing to say. I was little concerned with what should happen to me in the match. What worried me was that something would happen to Trumper which would prevent his playing. Although at that time I had never seen Trumper play, on occasions I had trudged from Waterloo across the sandhills to the Sydney Cricket Ground and waited at the gate to see the players come out. Once I had climbed on to a tram and actually sat opposite my hero for three stops. I would have gone farther, but having no money I did not want to take the chance of being kicked in the pants by the conductor. Even so I had gone half a mile out of my way.

In my wildest dreams I never thought I would even speak to Trumper–let alone play against him. I am fairly phlegmatic by nature but between the period of my selection and the match I must have behaved like a half-wit. Right up to my first Test match, I always washed and pressed my own flannels, but before this match I pressed them not once but several times. On the Saturday I was up with the sparrows and looking anxiously at the sky. It was a lovely morning but it still might rain. Come to that, lots of things could happen in two hours – there was still a chance that Vic might be taken ill or knocked down by a tram or twist his ankle or break his arm . . .

My thoughts were interrupted by a vigorous thumping on the back gate. I looked out of the washhouse-bathroom-woodshed-workshop window and saw that it was the milk-man who was kicking up the row. 'Hey,' he roared, 'yer didn't leave the can out. I can't wait round here all day. A man should pour it in the garbage tin – that'd make yer wake up a bit.' On that morning I wouldn't have cared whether he poured the milk in the garbage tin or all over me. I was playing against the great Victor Trumper. Let the milk take care of itself.

I kept looking at the clock. It might be slow – or it might have stopped. I'd better whip down to the Zetland hotel and check up. Anyway, I mightn't bowl at Trumper at all. He might get out before I come on. Or I mightn't get a bowl at all – I can't put myself on. Wonder what Trumper is doing this very minute . . . bet he's not ironing his flannels. Sends them to the laundry, I suppose. He's probably got two sets of flannels anyway. Perhaps he's at breakfast, eating bacon and eggs. Wonder if he knows I'm playing against him? Don't suppose he's ever heard of me. Wouldn't worry him anyhow, I shouldn't think. Gosh, what a long morning. Think I'll dig the garden. No, I won't. I want to keep fresh. Think I'll lie down for a bit . . . better not, I might fall off to sleep and be late.

The morning did not pass in this way. Time just stopped. I couldn't bring myself to do anything in particular and yet I couldn't settle to the thought of not doing anything. I was bowling to Trumper and I was not bowling to Trumper. I was early and I was late. In fact, I think I was partly out of my mind. I didn't get to the ground so very early after all, mainly because it would have been impossible for me

to wait around so near the scene of Trumper's appearance –
and yet for it to rain or news to come that something had
prevented Vic from playing.

'Is he here?' I asked Harry Goddard, our captain, the
moment I did arrive at the ground. 'Is who here?' he coun-
tered. My answer was probably a scornful and disgusted
look. I remember that it occurred to me to say, 'Julius
Caesar, of course,' but that I stopped myself being cheeky
because this was one occasion when I couldn't afford to be.

Paddington won the toss and took first knock. When
Trumper walked out to bat Harry Goddard said to me: 'I'd
better keep you away from Vic. If he starts on you he'll
probably knock you out of grade cricket.'

I was inclined to agree with him, yet at the same time I
didn't fear punishment from the master batsman. All I
wanted to do was just bowl at him. I suppose in their time
other ambitious youngsters have wanted to play on the same
stage with Henry Irving, or sing with Caruso or Melba, to
fight with Napoleon or sail with Columbus. It wasn't
conquest I desired. I simply wanted to meet my hero on
common ground. Vic, beautifully clad in creamy, loose-
fitting but well-tailored flannels, left the pavilion with his bat
tucked under his left arm and in the act of donning his
gloves. Although slightly pigeon-toed in the left foot he had
a springy athletic walk and a tendency to shrug his shoulders
every few minutes, a habit I understand he developed
through trying to loosen his shirt off his shoulders when it
became soaked with sweat during his innings.

Arriving at the wicket, he bent his bat handle almost to a
right angle, walked up the pitch, prodded about six yards of
it, returned to the crease and asked the umpire for 'two legs';
then he took a quick glance in the direction of fine leg,
shrugged again and took up his stance.

I was called to bowl sooner than I expected. I suspect now
that Harry Goddard changed his mind and decided to put me
out of my misery early in the piece. Did I ever bowl that
first ball? I don't remember. My mind was in a whirl. I really
think I fainted and the secret of that mythical first ball has

been kept over all these years to save me embarrassment. If the ball was sent down it must have been hit for six, or at least four, because I was awakened from my trance by that thunderous barracker Yabba booming, 'O for a strong arm and a walking stick!'

I do remember the next ball. It was, I imagined, a perfect leg-break. When it left my hand it was singing sweetly like a humming-top. The trajectory could not have been more graceful if designed by a professor of ballistics. The tremendous leg-spin caused the ball to swing and curve from the off and move in line with the middle and leg stump. Had I bowled this particular ball at any other batsman I would have turned my back early in its flight and listened for the death rattle. However, consistent with my idolatry of the champion, I watched his every movement. He stood poised like a panther ready to spring. Down came his left foot to within a foot of the ball. The bat, swung from well over his shoulders, met the ball just as it fizzed off the pitch and the next sound I heard was a rapping on the off-side fence. It was the most beautiful shot I have ever seen.

The immortal Yabba made some attempt to say something but his voice faded away to the soft gurgle one hears at the end of the kookaburra's song. The only person on the ground who didn't watch the course of the ball was Victor Trumper. The moment he played it he turned his back, smacked down a few tufts of grass and prodded his way back to the batting crease. He knew where the ball was going.

What were my reactions? Well, I never expected that ball or any other I could produce to get Trumper's wicket. But that being the best ball a bowler of my type could spin into being, I thought that at least Trumper might have been forced to play a defensive stroke, particularly as I was almost a stranger, too, and it might have been to his advantage to use discretion rather than valour. After I had bowled one or two other reasonably good balls without success I found fresh hope in the thought that Trumper had found Bosanquet, creator of the 'wrong-un' or 'bosie' (the latter, I think, a better name) rather puzzling. This left me with one shot in my locker, but if I didn't use it quickly I would be taken out of the firing line. I therefore decided to try this most undisciplined and cantankerous creation of the great Bosanquet – not, as many might think, as a compliment to the inventor but as the gallant farewell, so to speak, of a warrior who refused to surrender until all his ammunition was spent.

Again fortune was on my side in that I bowled the ball I had often dreamed of bowling. As with the leg-break, it had sufficient spin to curve in the air and break considerably after making contact with the pitch. If anything it might have had a little more top-spin, which would cause it to drop rather suddenly. The sensitivity of a spinning ball against the breeze is governed by the amount of spin imparted, and if a ball bowled at a certain pace drops on a certain spot, one bowled with identical pace but with more top-spin should drop eighteen inches or two feet shorter. For this reason I thought the difference in the trajectory and ultimate landing of the ball might provide a measure of uncertainty in Trumper's mind. While the ball was in flight this reasoning appeared to be vindicated by Trumper's initial movement. As at the beginning of my over, he sprang in to attack but did not realize that the ball, being an off-break, was floating away from him and dropping a little quicker.

In a split second Vic grasped this and tried to make up the deficiency with a wider swing of the bat. It was then I could see a passage-way to the stumps with our 'keeper, Con Hayes, ready to claim his victim. Vic's bat came through like a flash but the ball passed between his bat and legs, missed the stumps by a fraction, and the bails were whipped off with the great batsman at least two yards out of his ground.

Vic had made no attempt to scramble back. He knew the ball had beaten him and was prepared to pay the penalty, and although he had little chance of regaining his crease on this occasion I think he would have acted similarly if his back foot had been only an inch from safety.

As he walked past me he smiled, patted the back of his bat and said : 'It was too good for me.' There was no triumph in me as I watched the receding figure. I felt like a boy who had killed a dove.

Many of the cricketers of Trumper's period I came to know and even play with in those superb games we knew mid-week on the Sydney Cricket Ground No. 2. Hanson Carter, my first club captain, who saw much of Bradman, as did E. P. Barbour, and who toured Canada and the United States with the Don, used to say with great emphasis: 'Put Vic way up there [pointing to the sky] and then you can begin to talk of the others.' Carter also used to say sadly, 'There will never be another Victor.'

Charlie Macartney says he was one of the three most audacious and brilliant batsmen in Australian cricket – and cites his own innings in 1921 at Trent Bridge against Nottingham in which he scored 345 in under four hours. Macartney, who himself displayed much of the artistic wizardry and aggressiveness of Trumper, was reading the local newspaper next day and said to his fellows: 'It says here that my innings was reminiscent of Trumper. What rot! I wasn't fit to tie up Vic's laces as a batsman.'

Then there was an occasion when Trumper lifted George Hirst (one of the greatest left-hand bowlers of all time) over the square-leg fence. His skipper went down to Hirst who could only gasp and exclaim: 'But look at his legs. Look at his legs, right in front of the wicket.' 'Never mind his legs,' said the skipper, 'look at where the ruddy ball is.'

The purists were inclined to look upon Trumper with disfavour at first because he offended, as they thought, against basic batting principles. He didn't think that because a ball was pitched on the off, or stumps, that it couldn't be hit to leg, and this he did with impunity. Trumper obviously established his own conception of the batting art, and defence was no part of it – although it was said that as his career was drawing to a close he deferred to a more sober outlook. Like Bradman and Macartney he didn't believe there was a ball bowled that couldn't be hit somewhere. The tougher things were, the more problems there were, the better he liked it, often telling his struggling partner at the other end to leave it to him. Being at his best on 'sticky' wickets, he triumphed in the very wet season in England in 1902, hitting eleven centuries. At Old Trafford, in the fourth Test of that season, and one which Australia sensationally won by three runs, the Australians began the match on a wicket made soft by rain, although the run-up was so slippery that Lockwood could not bowl for over an hour. Archie MacLaren told his bowlers to keep Trumper quiet until lunch, and then the sun would affect the pitch. The start was delayed but at lunch the Australians were 173 for one, Trumper out for 104. When they grumbled at MacLaren for not keeping Trumper contained by field-placement, Mac-Laren, frustrated enough, exploded: 'Well, I couldn't put two fieldsmen in the practice-ground, could I?' To this day only Trumper, Macartney and Bradman have hit centuries before lunch in the Tests that really count, England v Australia, and that is fitting.

As I say, Trumper was at his best on 'stickies', and it is a pity that, with covered pitches and the gate to consider, these have gone out of the game. Noble said that perhaps Trumper's finest innings on a bad pitch was in Melbourne in 1904, against England, when he made 74 of a total of only 122. Such pitches when the ball flew at one's face or reared off a good length over one's head separated the men from the boys. Hobbs and Sutcliffe in later years were to conquer such pitches in Melbourne, but they called for skill as well as courage, for a Melbourne pitch with the sun on it is about as fierce as they come. Trumper was so severe on George Hirst, who must have dreamed of such a pitch on which to bowl his spinners, that he gave up bowling at the stumps and reverted to off-theory. Wilfred Rhodes, another great left-hand spinner, took fifteen wickets in the game, yet Noble records that Rhodes was so demoralized by Trumper's onslaught that he wouldn't bowl at the stumps, which he did to all the other batsmen, but kept the ball well wide of the off stump. 'That in itself,' says Noble, 'was the greatest compliment ever paid to Trumper.'

But the innings the NSW players of that time went into rhapsodies about was the one that Trumper played against

C

Victoria on the Sydney ground. Jack Saunders, a left-hander
whose natural viciousness was abetted by a wet pitch, had
dismissed four of NSW's best when Trumper came in. He beat
Trumper all ends up the first ball. 'All right, Jack,' Trumper
called down the pitch to him, 'I see what you are at. And I am
an old friend of yours. It is either you or me for it', and he
took out the long handle so effectively that he was 71 not out
at lunch and had a century soon afterwards. Carter says that
was the greatest innings he saw on a bad pitch, and Trumper's
185 not out against England at Sydney the best he'd seen on
a good one.

In their own playing time Grace, Trumper, Hobbs and Bradman were all cricketing legends. They did not have to wait
for time to hallow their names or mellow their deeds. One
could almost add the name of Sobers, the greatest all-rounder
of any age, but there were times when Sobers, who did not
apply himself to his art like the others, abdicated his throne.
Once, for instance, on the eve of a Sydney Test, he skipped a
nets session, pleading he had feet trouble, and went golfing
instead. There was another time, also on an Australian tour,
when Sobers, then captain of his team and with many problems
to solve, returned to Melbourne while his team went north to
Brisbane to prepare for the first Test. Thus I am not disposed
to put him on a similar pinnacle as the others: he didn't always
give the game his all.

Grace certainly did. Without any threat or usurpation he
ruled the cricket world of his time. Harry Altham, in his
absorbing *History of Cricket*, tells how in 1882 the critics had
written of the 'Old Man' – as Grace was affectionately known –
that time was beginning to pass him by, and that by the '90s
they saw him far past his best and dropping into the middle
background. Yet in May 1895 he performed the wonderful feat
of scoring a thousand runs in May. Grace had his own pitches
on matting at Crystal Palace, and he was always in good form
when the season began. In his first innings that 1895 season he
scored 13, then 103 for MCC against Sussex in the match
where Ranjitsinhji made his sensational début. There followed

two modest scores against Yorkshire and then – his 100th first-class hundred. The Doctor, on reaching three figures, only interrupted his innings to take a goodly swig of champagne, then went on to score 288. Next came a modest half-century against Cambridge. From there he travelled to Gravesend to play against Kent, and fielded while they went in first and made 470. He went in first for Gloucestershire and was last out for 257. He fielded again and saw Kent dismissed for 76, and then made 73 of the 104 needed for victory in 60 minutes of the 75 left for play. He was thus on the field for every ball bowled and made 330 runs for once out – all this by a heavily-built man at close on 47 years of age. On 30 May Grace won the toss for Gloucestershire against Middlesex at Lord's, chose to bat and got the 153 runs he needed for his 1000. All Lord's rose to him. Three separate testimonials – by MCC, his county and the *Daily Telegraph* – were started simultaneously for him, and the Doctor benefited by just on £10,000.

It was a pity that this marvellous athlete should have spoilt his image by some artful dodging on the field. He was often loath to go when out, and the Australians, though having a great personal liking for him, told many tales of his manipulation of umpires, most of whom stood in dread of him. Once, when he was bowled, he stooped, picked up the bails and replaced them, and said chattily to the umpire: 'Very windy today, umpire?' 'Yes,' said the umpire, 'very, but I'm not, and you're out and you are going.'

Undoubtedly, Jack Hobbs and Ranjitsinhji, both contemporaries of Trumper, are at the forefront of any discussion when the great batsmen of the world are mentioned. Ranji was a genius in what he attempted and did, and had a tremendous influence on classic batsmanship. Percy Fender, still living, told me once of how he played with Ranjitsinhji against the Australians for Sussex. (Percy, though few will know this, began his career with Sussex before transferring to Surrey.) The county were well up against it when Fender came out to bat. 'It was a source of wonderment to me,' said Fender. 'Ranji would talk with me at the end of the over when we were playing for him to keep the strike, and he would say: "I will play the next ball to the left hand of that man deep at leg. You be ready to run." And he never failed to do what he said he would.'

As for Jack Hobbs, he was admired and beloved by all. Altham says he was a man of great dignity and natural charm. He made 197 centuries, 98 of them after reaching the age of 40. He had a twinkle in his eyes that told of good humour and he had a natural modesty that was captivating. Chatting with him one would never guess that he was the Great Hobbs. Many of his best innings, like Trumper's, were played on difficult pitches, on which he was, indeed, the Master. His career spanned great opening partners from Tom Hayward to Andy Sandham, and he shared in 23 Test partnerships of over 100, eight of them with Rhodes, fifteen with Sutcliffe. I had a letter recently from an Australian, Jack McAtamney, who saw all Hobbs's greatest innings and still plumps for him as the greatest. McAtamney had run into Bertie Oldfield in a Sydney street some six months before Oldfield died, and he told Bertie that Jack had written of him that Oldfield never appealed unless he thought the batsman was out. Oldfield replied: 'Dear gentleman Jack. It was always a joy to play against him – just to watch his footwork.' Stan McCabe also told me that he learned more about the art of batting by watching the footwork of Hobbs in a short innings against the 1930 Australians at the Oval than in all the rest of his career.

Trumper was the idol of the crowd wherever he played in England or Australia. So was Bradman. English crowds revered them both. It is unavoidable that the two should be compared, and many did not hesitate to do this. They come down hard on Trumper's side, admitting on statistics that Bradman was a street ahead, but that Trumper had about his batting an art, a consummate poetry of motion and an ability to do well on 'stickies' that the younger man did not approach. In *Farewell to Cricket* Bradman, who seems to answer every criticism, no matter how slight, compares his rate of centuries to Trumper's. He wrote:

> I do not want to enter into a discussion about Trumper, but perhaps in fairness to myself I may say this. If the argument is used that big scores were responsible for my average, then surely scores of up to 100 only would not come into it. In that regard Trumper's record in England disclosed 19 centuries in 193 innings, mine was 41 centuries in 120 innings. On a percentage basis, Trumper got one century for every 9.8 innings, where I obtained one century every 3.4.

I could answer some of the Don's criticisms and observations, and indeed later in this book I will do so; at the moment it is enough to say that both Trumper and Bradman, one before the other and possibly setting standards, were an adornment to cricket. They gave terrific entertainment and enjoyment wherever they played.

Though we never knew him personally, lads of my generation knew all about Trumper. In the torrid and turgid discussions over cricket – to which we listened on the outskirts of the circle with intense wonderment, silence and respect – Trumper's name was always being mentioned. The old sages of the game would have nobody included in the same breath. Kippax, whom we knew well, was only a pale imitation, they said, of the real champion, and Kippax was a classic batsman.

I have heard many tales of Trumper but it is hard to check them now. One was supposed to have been told to Charlie Trumper (Vic's brother) by J. J. Kelly, the wicket-keeper, whose sister-in-law Victor married. It was at Lord's, and the great Dr W. G. Grace was supposed to have walked the length of the Pavilion to seek Trumper out in the Australian dressing-room. He said to Trumper, 'Bring me your bat.' Victor did so. W.G. then handed him a fountain-pen and said, 'Sign it.' Trumper did, and W.G. then said, 'Give it to me,' and Trumper did so. W.G. handed him his own autographed bat and said, 'From the reigning champion to the future champion,' and without more ado stalked back to the English room.

It is a pretty story, but on checking the scores in Irving Rosenwater and Ralph Barker's splendid book, *England v. Australia*, I find that Grace had been dropped for the Lord's match in an English home Test side for the first time, so the alleged facts must be dubious. Trumper and the English colossus played against each other in only one Test, the first of 1899 at Trent Bridge. Grace made 28 and 1 and Trumper was clean bowled by Jack Hearne in the first innings for nil and the second innings by Jackson for 11. They did, however, play again against each other at Lord's at the end of July 1899, when MCC played the Australians. By then Trumper had made his great Lord's Test century and the 300 at Hove, so the story *could* stand up.

Oscar Wilde once wrote there is always something about your success that displeases even your best friends, but that could not be said of Trumper. He was the only cricketer I knew or heard of, with one exception, against whom I never heard a word of criticism or a begrudging word. Strudwick once criticized his technique on the leg stump.

As well as being immortal as a batsman, his character and personality were flawless. Everybody loved him, even the bowlers he carved into small pieces. He was always considerate of his team-mates and gave no thought to himself. A little incident during his Testimonial match in Sydney typified his kindly nature. He slipped out of the dressing-room, out of the entrance gate, and walked several hundred yards along the back of the ground to the entrance to the Hill. He had a pocketful of minute threepenny pieces ('tray bits', as we knew them) and he handed them out one by one to the small urchins who were waiting there for him. He had come so often before. The entrance to the Hill in those days was 1/- for adults and 3d for children. No wonder Trumper always got a great cheer when he appeared!

I have mentioned Eric McElhone in my Acknowledgements. Eric's wife was the sister-in-law of the late E. A. (Chappie)

Dwyer, the former Australian selector and one of Australia's most popular officials. He managed Lindsay Hassett's Australian team to South Africa after the Second World War, but unfortunately he never took a team to England. Chappie lived at the rear of Trumper's home in Paddington and was one of the many local boys who used to bowl against Trumper in a lane that ran behind their homes. 'We didn't think much of Trumper,' he told me once, 'and frequently bowled him out, even after he had made a big score that day on the Sydney Cricket Ground.' That was typical of Trumper – to have a knock with the boys although he had been playing cricket all day, and then to let them bowl him out. Imagine the thrill!

Again, Sir William McKell, the sometime Governor-General, tells how, as one of a band of small boys, he used to follow Trumper all round Sydney when he was playing club cricket. Transport was not easy to get then and they often used to 'scale' their way to the various grounds, risking an early brush with authority to see their revered champion.

> He never let us down. He gave us enough to talk about for the whole week. I remember, once, when Victor had set up a sports-goods shop, going with my other cobbers to buy what we called a 'compo' ball. It cost a whole sixpence. Victor sent us on our way with a whole cricketing set, two bats, stumps, bails, pads, the whole lot, and all it cost was the sixpence for the 'compo' ball. No wonder he was our hero! We venerated him.

'Scale', by the way, was a term used to describe the method of one who went places on Sydney's trams (now all gone) on the cheap. He evaded fares by hopping on when the conductor wasn't looking and off when he was. This led to a great battle of tactics between the conductor and armies of small boys. The boys of those days were adept in hopping on to the footboard of a tram, using the hand-grips at the side. Sometimes, when they missed their footing or grip through misjudgement, they went underneath the tram. There was thus great risk, and skill, in travelling on the trams. The agility of Sydney news-boys, who could join or leave a tram facing backwards, was incredible.

Trumper did not care about money. The tales of his generosity are legion. He was a bad businessman when he set up shop in the sporting world, and gave many goods away to the needy. When his famous NSW and Australian partner, Reggie Duff, died in penury, Trumper had a whip-round among his fellows for Duff's funeral. He didn't collect enough – and promptly put in the balance himself. Syd Smith, who managed two Australian teams to England, was one of the trustees of the funds from Trumper's Testimonial match. Vic was such an easy 'touch' that they felt they could not trust him with the money, from which they formed a fund and paid his widow a monthly cheque. It was wise. The day after the match finished a man came to the fundraisers with a note from Trumper saying that the bearer once used to work for him, binding bats. He was now in monetary difficulties and would the Trust give him £60? At that rate the Testimonial money would quickly have disappeared!

Such stories of Trumper are legion, though some have an edge. One London night, after the team had been to a theatre, Trumper noticed a small boy huddled from the rain and selling sheets of music. Trumper left his fellows, took some money out of his pocket, bought the lot, and sent the grateful child home. He then put the sheets in a rubbish bin.

'Recorded centuries leave no trace/On memory of that time-less grace' wrote that excellent literary all-rounder John Arlott. Yet perhaps Harry Altham best summed up Trumper in *The World of Cricket*. 'The measure of Trumper's genius', he wrote, 'is not to be found in any figures: it was essentially qualitative rather than quantitative, revealed in terms of spontaneous art rather than in any acquired technique. He had the lissom and co-ordinated body of a natural athlete; like all great batsmen he seemed to sight the ball as soon as it left the bowler's hand, and he moved into his strokes with effortless and perfectly balanced ease. There was no limit to their range, or flaw in their fluency or timing; the better the bowling, the more difficult the wicket, the more likely was his genius to rise to the challenge.'

He was, as one might term it, the original Greek of batting. Like the Greeks in their language, Trumper was particularly fitted in power and precision for the immortal expression of beautiful stroke play and presence at the crease. The Greeks would have made another god of him. He came, too, at an important time in Australian history, at a time of Federation, and he and Dame Nellie Melba and Les Darcy were the other great Australians of that time to bring Australia the world-wide notoriety it sought as a young nation anxious to impress.

Finally, a story told me by Jimmy Sullivan – long a member of one of Trumper's Sydney clubs, Gordons – and illustrative of how Trumper stood in the national consciousness. It concerns Loretto Convent, Kirribilli, where my second daughter, Jacquelyn, was educated. The nuns hit on the idea of having the girls say for school prayers the ones they said at home. Each boarder was to take it in turn and there was the usual string of 'God bless Mummy and Daddy', and then uncles and aunts and those stricken by illness. One girl staggered all as she finished with 'And, please God, bless Victor Trumper.'

2

Paddington

It is well to know the strong feeling of nationalism that was arising in Australia around Trumper's time and how his great deeds and fame fed the flames.

Historians of Australia are divided in their opinions as to whether the bush, the goldfield or the city contributed most to the formation of the Australian national identity in the nineteenth century. They are also divided as to the relative contribution of indigenous and imported British characteristics. Discussion so far has largely ignored one aspect of Australia that can hardly be itself in dispute – the country's concern with sport. Australia's national heroes are largely cricketers, tennis-players, swimmers, boxers – even racehorses. Probably only Ned Kelly (the infamous bushranger) and the largely nameless heroes of ANZAC rival in the public imagination those who have gained fame in the sports arena or on the racetrack. Phar Lap would rate more highly than any politician, Don Bradman more than any artist.

Cricket in Australia, played at an international level since 1861, has provided more heroes than any other single sport, from Spofforth and Murdoch, through Trumper and Bradman, down to Lillee. Its national teams, particularly in their contests with England, have given the nation a yardstick to measure its strength. This chapter will attempt to show that a study of Australia's cricketing history in the nineteenth century, and of the contemporary opinions expressed about that history, can add something to a tale normally told through a study of politics, literature, or similar more conventional aspects of social history.

*

Cricket was played continually at an international level from the 1860s onwards. Scullers, boxers, wrestlers and rifle-shooters appeared sporadically to meet and often beat their rivals from the old world and the new, but cricket was unique in having a continuous international history, and, what is more, it was played against England, which gave the struggle a particular piquancy.

There were four phases in the development of Australia's cricketing nationalism. At first, in the 1860s, when the two English sides visited Australia, the attitudes expressed were those of humility and deference. The colonials were aware of their deficiencies, hoped to learn from their visitors, and looked upon them with affection and respect. By the mid-1870s a change had taken place. Australians felt, with justice, that their cricket had improved and that England could be beaten. They were right, and the victories, first of her XVIIIs, then of her XIs, were hailed as showing that on both the narrow stage of cricket itself and, by extension, on the wider arena of national physical and moral development, Australians had nothing to fear from either their origins or their location 'south of the line'.

The late '70s and '80s were times of mixed feelings. Some were proud that victories over Englishmen showed Australian strength, others that they confirmed that Australians were still basically English. Lack of success in the later 1880s and the nature of Australian touring teams to England, which were criticized for being too mercenary, tended to make this a slack phase in the development of cricketing nationalism, but in the '90s a revival of interest, coupled with some crushing victories, gave Australia a sense of cricketing confidence, even arrogance, that was held up as an example of what federation and co-operation might do and what nationhood had already achieved.

The drawing of wider parallels from the examples of manly sports, especially from cricket, was an Anglo-Saxon habit in the nineteenth century, and the assertion that ability at cricket indicated national superiority was commonplace. Thus the *Quarterly Review* of October 1857 compared the games-playing

English public schoolboy with 'the pale-faced student of Germany, or the over-taught pupil of (the) French polytechnique'. The Englishman had nothing to fear from them: games had given him 'pluck, blood, and bottom'. Charles Box, writing in the 1870s, asked:

> Who could, for instance, picture to his imagination the phlegmatic Dutchman, with his capacious round stern, chasing or sending the ball whizzing through the air like a cannon shot, and getting a run with the speed of a roebuck? [Charles Box had no inkling then that these 'round-sterned' Dutchmen were once to beat Lawry's Australians in Holland when they broke across from an Australian tour of England!] The idea even appears beyond the pale of conception. The effete inhabitants of cloudless Italy, Spain and Portugal would sooner face a solid square of British infantry than an approaching ball from the sinewy arms of a first-class bowler. Instead of the bat, their backs would be turned for the purpose of stopping it.

Mr Box could well have had a premonition about Australian backs during the bodyline imbroglio, or even English backs against Lillee and Thomson!

Another author suggested of cricket that 'to question its perfect blessedness is analagous to questioning the perfect blessedness of being born and bred a Briton'; and Major Philip Trevor stated that 'when you find a man completely out of sympathy with cricket you will generally find some other rather un-English trait in his character'.

Cricket was brought to Australia by British settlers, soldiers and sailors, and as the game grew in popularity in England in the 1840s and 1850s so it did in Australia. Interest was high but standards were low. Cricket matches were often largely an excuse for 'nobblerizing' (I'm afraid many still are): one writer rebuked a correspondent who had claimed cricket was played with more spirit in the colonies than in England: 'What does he mean? I have it. More nobblers and shandygaff; he is right.' Australian cricketers did not have to contend only with the hazards induced by alcohol. Cattle and goats browsed in the outfield of the Melbourne Cricket Ground in the 1850s and at Ballarat cricket was played on a pitch that was not level in any single place. The Domain, Sydney's major cricket ground, was a public park that lacked the facilities of an enclosed ground. Equipment was primitive. The game was generally played barefoot and seems to have justified a retrospective judgement that prior to the first English visit Australian cricket was 'decidedly colonial, agricultural and uncouth'.

It was this combination of keenness coupled with a justified sense of deficiency that coloured Australian attitudes to the first touring side. The English team, brought out by the Melbourne caterers, Spiers and Pond, arrived to a tumultuous and extra-ordinary reception in December 1861. The Colonial press and public were both deferential and enthusiastic. The Englishmen, it was said, were there to show the Australians 'perfection', and no player need to feel 'humiliation if he is vanquished'. The thought that NSW could come off victorious in a cricket-ing contest with All England was laughed to scorn at a Sydney reception where the prospect of defeat for the Englishmen was reckoned as likely as that of English soldiers being beaten. The English side did, in fact, lose two up-country matches but was clearly immeasurably superior to anything Australia could offer. Victoria and NSW (who seldom agreed on anything) agreed on the success of the tour, and newspapers piously lectured their readers on the importance to Australians of learning and emulation.

Two years later, in the summer of 1863–4, a second team arrived, again of professionals, though including a single amateur, E. M. Grace. It won all its games, but was less fervently received than its predecessors. The money-grabbing behaviour of many of its members, who brought cricket equip-ment with them to sell, were avid for gifts or cheap purchases of gold and jewellery, and who also showed a decided predelic-tion for champagne luncheons, fine dinners and first-class hotels, excited unfavourable comment.

A fully professional English side, after the financial and social excesses of that team, was unwelcome for a long interval, and it was considered that an amateur side would be either too costly or too weak. An expatriate Cambridge blue, W. J. Hammersley, wrote in *The Australasian* of 15 July 1871 that an amateur team would be useless; it might have 'spotless flannels, gorgeous stripes and caps [Australians have long continued since then to be suspicious of what they call coloured caps], the neatest thing in gloves and pads, snowy white shoes, and all that, with big buckles and flaming neckties; but what would the play be?' Already a down-to-earth tone was becoming observable in Australian attitudes and, later in the same piece, Hammersley, who wrote under the name 'Long Stop', sneered at a swell with a string of Christian names beginning with 'Edward Wolryke Orlando' getting a 'duck's egg'.

It is interesting that 'Long Stop' felt Australian cricket deserved worthwhile opposition. The visits of the English teams, the engagement of English coaches, and the migration of skilled amateur cricketers to Australia were held largely responsible for the transformation of the late 1860s and early 1870s. The Australian press was generous in its praises to such men, and reminded readers : 'We must never forget how much we owe to the home polish, how much indebted we are to men who learnt their cricket in the Old Country.' This attitude was to condition much of the thinking and influence much of the debate during the second phase of the development of Australian cricketing nationalism, that of the 1870s, when some highly complex and ambivalent views were expressed, the main arguments being for and against acknowledging the supremacy of English teams when clearly their Australian counterparts were burgeoning into a status of their own.

Such was the general picture of Australian cricket when Victor Trumper arrived on the scene. Australians, never loath to boast of their many outstanding sporting deeds, were to have in him a man who established new precepts of the game, who was to express a commanding Australian nationalism never before experienced, and who was to win the love and affection of everybody with whom he came in contact, both in England and Australia.

We can now turn to his particular background.

*

The early Sydney pioneers didn't show much originality in their naming of streets and places. The suburb Paddington was obviously named after the London railway station. A paper published by the Paddington municipal council says the suburb had no history in so far as history consists of battle and bloodshed, and Paddington's history, it proudly stresses, is a record of the birth and growth of communities and towns. In a burst of municipal pride the council states that it can safely challenge the world to a comparison. I doubt the world took up the challenge.

The borough is one which in its rapid and sound growth can win the admiration of all other cities in the state. The wilderness of scrub, rock and sand has been changed in a little more than the allotted life of man into a stately town. We have a history which by the energy and the civic spirit of the people is one unbroken record of advancement and success and is but the first stage in a triumphal development into a model city.

The foundations of Paddington were laid in 1838 when the inevitably named 'Victoria Barracks' were begun. They were made from stone quarried on the ground and the quarrymen were a party of Canadians transported to Australia for rebellion. The government masons were chosen from England to maintain the balance of population in the colony which was then already coloured by the Irish and Scots. The extensive buildings at the barracks caused quite an influx of residents into Paddington, and the contractors for the barracks also erected a number of houses in the district – some wood, some stone; shops also were erected to cater for the soldiers. The first pub was built in 1855. The barracks were also finished in 1855, during the governorship of Sir George Gipps, and were first occupied by the 11th Regiment under Colonel Bloomfield. They continue to this day, a magnificent collection of old, solid, stone buildings.

Paddington is only a short distance from the city proper, but some of the soldiers then were indignant at being sent to the barracks at Paddington from George Street. They said they were being sent into the 'interior' of Australia. There was a great deal of grumbling. They said they would never be able to get into the bright lights of the city at night-time and they objected strongly to having to live in the scrub. The 'Iron Duke', the first omnibus to run from the city to Paddington, first ran in 1853, and was driven by a famous character named 'Old Steve'. Its terminus was at the Paddington Inn at the corner of Oxford and William streets.

Two years later, in 1855, C. McClutchy started another bus from the city to Paddington, the fare being 1/- each way. McClutchy also made up parties on moonlit nights and drove to South Head. Sometimes these buses also ran in the day-time, along dusty, rough tracks, and were very popular with home-sick Britishers who loved to sit at South Head and gaze at the incoming waves crashing on to the cliffs, imagining the waves were coming from the old country as they looked out to sea. They had vivid imaginations.

The early Paddington people must have been made of the stuff that counts. The buses used then were low-roofed, narrow and with straight sides, and for seats pieces of board, little more than six inches wide, were placed down and across the buses. The state of the 'roads' along which the buses had to pass made the journey to Paddington from the city a series of jumps, bumps, roots and tree stumps, so that the discomfort of a bus ride in such circumstances was much easier imagined than described. At this time there were upon the market and freely sold in Paddington several new nostrums in the shape of liniments and ointments highly extolled for bruises received in the use of the Iron Duke; Old Steve – once a week it was said – could be relied upon to deposit his live cargo on the muddy banked-up sidewalk.

I can personally remember, in the middle of the twenties, when a bus trip between Bondi Junction and the Railway was a thrill a minute. Conductors would over-fill their buses at the Junction and, with two or even three buses setting out for the city simultaneously, it was a rare battle of speed and manoeuvring to get first to an intermediate stop where the conductor, who possibly spent his early days in a sardine factory, would pile on yet more customers.

Then came the big test of the skill of the driver, down Oxford Street and past the Barracks to Darlinghurst, where another batch of passengers would be waiting. The main point was to get in front of a tram so that progress would not be impeded down the Barracks hill. This often involved spurting past on the wrong side, and those within the crowded, swaying bus would hold their collective breath and hope for a safe arrival at Darlinghurst. Sometimes one would do the trip from the Junction to the railway in seven or eight minutes, the normal time being half an hour; but if you had the heart and the mind for the trip you were well recompensed, although often it seemed we would emulate Old Steve and finish on the footpath or hit an oncoming tram. One advantage we did have over Old Steve: our bus had springs over its axles.

Paddington is now the centre of Sydney's sporting complex. It embraces the Cricket Ground, the Sports Ground and the Royal Agricultural showground, while on its outskirts are the magnificent Randwick racecourse, Centennial Park, and the lawn tennis courts at Rushcutters Bay where the Davis Cup has been played, while its fringe touches several golf clubs. Also, of course, there are other municipal cricket grounds, including the old Hampden Oval.

Sydney was founded on a portion of a rock promontory between Darling Harbour and the Tank Stream. In the early days the surrounding country was most uninviting, being composed mostly of sand, hills, or hummocks covered with scrub. The spread of the settlement east was forced through the necessity of finding a road by land to the pilot station established at South Head. It is quite possible that an extension of the settlement in that direction was also considered as early as when the First Fleet arrived in 1788. Sheds had been erected on the barren shores to protect the stores, huts had been built for the convicts, and soldiers and officials were living under canvas. Gangs of men were sent into the woods to cut timber and others were sent farther afield to a swamp at the head of a small bay to cut rushes for roofs and bedding

D

for the horses.

It is reported that the aborigines had become incensed at the attention paid by the white men to their gins (women), and took revenge on the first white men they found away from their fellows. Six convicts engaged in cutting rushes and guarded by two soldiers were set upon by a large party of aborigines and speared to death. The scrub and hills afforded special shelter for this kind of warfare. When news of the attack was reported to the Governor he christened the scene 'Rushcutters Bay'. Overlooking that pleasant bay now is the modern motel at which English cricketers stay when they are in Sydney.

Hampden Oval was an old quarry and garbage dump which was built up as much as thirteen feet in places to make the cricket oval. It was called after Viscount Hampden, the then NSW Governor, and was one of the main reasons why M. A. Noble wanted Trumper to play with the Paddington club. A great demonstration of Paddington togetherness accompanied the ground's opening. Owners of produce stores gave bags of potatoes, butchers in the district gave a sheep each, bakers gave bread and grocers gave jams and tea. A bullock was roasted whole and various games were held – such as catching the pig by the tail and climbing the greasy pole, as well as a fancy-dress cricket match, in which Trumper played. The new fire brigade, the pride and joy of the district, came along to lend colour to the occasion, but coming down Glenmore Road it toppled over with its horses and a man was seriously injured.

Eventually the day got out of hand. Hogsheads of beer had been donated by various breweries, and the beer was free. The committee found, however, that many were inclined to 'consume more than was needed for their welfare', so they stopped the supply of beer and the surplus was poured down the gutters of Glenmore Road. But all Paddington agreed it was a red-letter day that opened Hampden Oval.

3
Early Days

The Trumpers were originally an English family. Charles, Victor's father, was born in London, and even at one stage emigrated to New Zealand before settling in Australia. He was a short man with a goatee beard, sparkling eyes, and a keen sense of humour. He married Louise Coughlan, who was three years older than him, and together they had eight children, of whom Victor was the first. Then followed Alice, who died on her 21st birthday, May Trumper (subsequently Mrs Nicholas), Una (subsequently Mrs George Smith), Sidney, born 1893, and Charles Ernest, born 1899. Una was the mother of a man later to become one of Australia's service leaders, Admiral Sir Victor Alfred Trumper Smith, KBE, CB, DSC. Two more girls died in infancy.

Victor's parents brought up their young family at 112 Paddington Street, Paddington, one of the many terrace houses in the district. It is about 300 yards north of Oxford Street, one of the main arteries in Sydney, running from the city out to the eastern suburbs and leading on to the famed Bondi. Paddington, which is next to Woollahra, which in turn is next to the better-known Waverley, is now one of the most fashionable suburbs of Sydney, having grown from a densely populated working-class suburb into one in which the old Victorian terrace houses are eagerly sought and their interiors modernized, while the lattice iron-work on the old balconies are collectors' pieces. It is today at the heart of Sydney's art world.

The Trumper house would have been typical of the ordinary working man's home in those days – no wireless, no television, and no abundance of money, but peaceful and contented. Charles Trumper played the piano – as did Victor – and the house often resounded to song as the Trumpers and their neighbours gathered round for a sing-song.

The suburban folk of those days were a generous lot. If a breadwinner died the district would organize a testimonial concert to meet the costs of the funeral, and the items would all be contributed by neighbours. I remember going to one of these concerts during the early war years in Paddington. Many of the items were of the tear-jerker variety, as songs of those days seemed mostly to be. I remember a young lass singing 'Please give me a penny, sir, a penny please for bread; oh, I'm so hungry, sir, a penny please for bread,' and the coins rained in on to the stage.

Although Trumper senior loved cricket and transmitted that love to his son, it was not until Trumper went to Crown Street Superior Public School – 'Public School', in this instance, differing from the Public Schools of England – that he began to shoot ahead at the game. Noble, five years older than Trumper, was in his final year when Trumper came and interest in cricket was already high. Each summer the boys would eat their lunch hurriedly and then it was cricket, and in double quick time. Whoever caught the batsman or bowled him was next in, and Trumper once batted for six weeks. His father would occasionally ask him how he was getting on and Trumper would reply, 'I am still in.' It was from this that Trumper senior realized his son's potential in cricket and took a greater interest in his game.

Victor was also fond of Rugby, and after leaving school played with the South Sydney Rugby Football Club. However, after breaking his collar bone at this game he realized there was more future for him in cricket and gave up actively playing. Even so, he never lost his love for football and was at the inaugural meeting of the Rugby League code, which was held in his shop when he went into business. Trumper was also the League's first Treasurer.

The modern attractions of surfing and motoring were not 'on' in those days for schoolboys, and in their holidays or after school the boys would play cricket or football in the open fields, in lanes or in back-yards. From this type of cricket they developed an alert eye to jab down on 'shooters' or 'grubbers',

112 Paddington Street
'Home of the immortal Victor Trumper'

Cedric Emanuel

and learnt to get out of the way against kicking balls; it was
this experience which undoubtedly led to Trumper being
proficient on 'stickies'.

At that time there was a huge field on the eastern side of the
concrete path leading from Moore Park Road to the northern
entrance to the Sydney Cricket Ground and extending in an
easterly direction to near Centennial Park. Here the boys played
friendly matches on Saturday mornings as well as whenever
else they could. The area, known as 'Red Pitch' from the colour
of the soil, was no great distance from the Trumper home.
Trumper would also practise both in Surry Hills and in his
own back-yard for hours every day, swinging his bat until it
almost seemed part of him, making his strokes, without a ball,
like a boxer shadow-sparring, and using his feet in pre-
conceived strokes. 'When I saw to what extent he had pro-
gressed I would encourage him in every possible way,' said
his father. 'Early every morning I would go with him to a
concrete pitch on Moore Park and bowl to him. We would
remain there from six a.m. to eight a.m., and only knock off
on account of the fact that I had to go to business and Victor
to school. It was surprising to note the rapid headway he made
as a result of his constant practice. Every day I would note
some degree of improvement in his skill with the bat and in
his style of play.'

Trumper's fame with Crown Street was spreading, and his
presence in the school side attracted much attention at their
matches. Many older men, as they watched, knew they were
seeing a future champion. When in 1894 Andrew Stoddart's
English team visited Australia they invited the keen boys of
the Paddington area to bowl against them at the Cricket Ground
nets, and put 2/- on the stumps to encourage them. If the boys
hit the stumps the 2/- was theirs, while the Englishmen got
much good practice. Net bowlers, I should explain, are always
at a premium on any tour. Tour bowlers are usually weary
and chary of bowling against batsmen they might later oppose
in county games – Grimmett and O'Reilly, for instance, were
always careful not to give an early display of their wares to
batsmen from another State. Trumper was a more than fair

medium-fast bowler when he was young, and would have been good practice for the Englishmen. His fellows mentioned to the touring team Trumper's prowess with the bat and the English-men sometimes invited him to show his skill. This he did to such a marked degree against Lockwood, Richardson, Peel and Briggs that the Englishmen expressed the opinion even then that Trumper would one day be the best batsman in the world.

Bill Whitty, also an Australian player, was another young-ster to bowl at the Cricket Ground nets. In his book *80 Not Out* Les Hill tells how Trumper pushed Whitty's claims and was invited by Mr George Barbour, father of Eric, to bowl against the *Sydney Grammar School*, where Barbour was a master. He was also invited to bowl against I Zingari, a club team comprised of barristers and doctors and such, of Sydney. One day Whitty got a call when he was bowling in the nets against Sydney Grammar to come to the other Cricket Ground nets and bowl against the NSW cricketers. For this occasion, as Whitty relates, he dressed himself smartly in his best cricket-ing gear. He wore his only pair of creams freshly ironed, his best white shirt and football boots, which he freshly white-washed. He bowled his heart out at great players like Trumper, Noble, Duff, Kelly, Carter and Cotter, little thinking that in two years he would be playing Test cricket with them. Alick Bannerman, frequenting the nets with his brother Charlie, spoke to Whitty: 'Son, I think you can play this game a bit. But let me give you a word of advice. Try to look the part.' Poor Whitty then realized that his whitewashed football boots were not quite the thing. Whitty, who came from Newtown, later migrated to South Australia and had more success against Trumper than any other bowler. He was also one of Trumper's best mates. I intended to go to Tantanoola on my way to Adelaide once to cover a Test match and have a talk with Whitty, who obviously could have told me much about Trumper; but a few days before my arranged visit I had a nice letter from Mary, Bill's wife, saying that her husband, although anxious to give me as much help as he could, was sadly past it. He died a few days later. He was the last Australian player of that era.

Trumper senior is the authority for stating that Victor never played in Sydney junior cricket. When he was fourteen he went on a visit to an uncle in Bulli down the south coast, and while there was invited to play against Mount Keira. Strangely, he starred as a bowler, taking almost the whole of the opposition wickets for 19 runs. Trumper's father also remembered the first game of cricket his son played against older men. One Saturday afternoon when he was a boy in knickerbockers young Trumper was passing through Moore Park where a match was about to be played between the second elevens of the Carlton and Warwick clubs. Carlton were short of a man and as soon as Trumper was sighted he was asked to fill the vacancy. This he consented to do and opened the eyes of watchers as, though so small a boy, he made 24 runs and took eight wickets with his bowling.

His father proudly told of the reputation his son was making in those circles around Moore Park, a famous nursery for cricketers. Vic agreed to take part in another match with Carlton but when the opposing side saw that Victor was to play they refused to start the game. Trumper senior regarded this as an extraordinary tribute to his son's prowess as, with the exception of Trumper, the teams were composed of grown men. However, in the Australian Cricket Annual of 1896 J. C. Davis ('Not out' of the *Sydney Referee*, the undisputed cricket critic of those days), said that in 1894–5 Trumper was 12th of the 13 batsmen of the club, and that his figures were: 12 innings, 1 not out, highest score 22 not out, aggregate 107 runs at an average of 9·72. He was, seemingly, fortunate to have held his position. He seems also to have spent the previous season with the South Sydney seconds, but that side's only mention for that season was that they finished in last position, so they could not have had many stars, if any.

With a view to giving special encouragement to rising cricketers, the SCG gave membership to all schoolboys and undergraduates of the University at a special fee of half a guinea. This gave such members use of all practice facilities and admission to all pavilions. In addition schools were offered the chance to use a special net for the summer at £7 10s, but the Sydney Grammar School, as it was nearby, was the only school to take advantage of this. Trumper himself says in an article personally written by him for *C. B. Fry's Magazine* in 1905 that he was still at school at Crown Street when he was first selected to represent NSW against South Australia.

In 'A chat with Victor Trumper', published in *Boys' Own Paper* of 1905, Trumper is alleged to have said that he was educated at the Sydney Grammar School. He was not; he was always at Crown Street. His brothers, Sid and Charlie, were educated at Sydney Grammar School, but not Victor. This confusion came about possibly because he practised with them, as did Whitty, at their SCG net.

After leaving school Trumper became for a while an assistant teacher. After that he worked as a clerk in the Government Printing Office, then worked with Tom Garrett, Registrar of Probates and Curator of Intestate Estates, a former Australian great bowler. Garrett took Trumper under his wing and secured for him a position in his office. From here Trumper left to open his sports-goods store in Sydney in the early 1900s. Trumper was loath for a number of years to go into the sporting goods business because Syd Gregory was also in that business and Trumper did not want to tread on his toes. Even after he had conquered these scruples he showed, like his father, who opened a slipper factory and did not succeed in it, that he had little business acumen. Late one day for a match Trumper took a bat out of stock, hit a century with it, and returned it to stock – marked at half price because it was second hand! Trumper also had a tie shop in Sydney. His first sports shop was in Hunter Street, later on the northern side of Market Street, where David Jones's store now stands. The last of his three sports-goods shops was in George Street, where Wynyard Station is now sited.

In 1908 his parents moved from Paddington to a new home in Help Street, Chatswood, on the western side of Chatswood Station and not far from it. They bought an old stone cottage with a good frontage and a big block of land on it upon which Trumper senior built several cottages. Victor by now was married. He was married on 7 June 1904, to Sarah Ann Briggs.

She was a sister of the wife of J. J. Kelly, the Australian wicket-keeper of those days, and Trumper met her apparently during his many visits to Melbourne, when he stayed with Kelly.

Trumper had two children, Ann Louise, who was aged about nine when Trumper died, and who died herself from leukaemia when aged 50, and a boy, Victor junior, who was only sixteen months old when his dad died. Trumper took his wife to live with his parents in Surry Hills and Paddington and they moved with them to Chatswood. In other words, in his married life, Trumper lived always with his parents and it was possible that the money he made from tours to England helped his father to buy the Chatswood property. It was likely, too, that Trumper, often absent from home on cricket tours, reasoned that his wife would have company with his parents.

The big property in Chatswood had much land and the Trumpers built a turf pitch in the garden. Here Charlie Macartney, living nearby and one of the Trumpers' most constant friends, practised with him often in the early morning and late afternoon. But that was after Trumper's brilliant days with Paddington.

In the *Town and Country Journal* of 29 January 1913 S. H. Bowden gives a good insight into Trumper's early days:

Some 20 years ago [Trumper would then have been 16] on the Sydney Domain a match was played between the Carlton and Warwick clubs. The trundling of the veteran Ted Evans was negotiated for by a slim youngster who met every ball with the full face of an impeccably straight bat which dealt with anything off the wicket if not in a powerful yet in an irreproachably artistic manner. Said Evans: 'That youngster, given opportunity, will develop into a world batsman.' Charles Bannerman, in his day one of Australia's most brilliant batsmen, evidently thought so too for he at once took this lad, Victor Trumper, under his cricketing aegis and by precepts and example instilled into him the fundamental principles of our grand old game.

Time after time we have been at the nets at the Association Cricket Ground, noting Charlie, the champion who had

been instructing Victor, the champion of the future. For a
time all went well, but young Trumper, having mastered the
defensive tactics of the game, began to do a little original
work in the most daring of strokes. In vain would Bannerman call out: 'Leave it alone, Vic. That wasn't a ball to go
at.' Victor 'went' at all such deliveries and, more than once,
made off with them, making scoring strokes with consummate ease. After a while the old coach very wisely left the
young batsman to his own devices. Sam Jones, Harry Moses
and several other top-notchers of those days, with foresight
based on insight, also saw Trumper and 'named a star'.

But it is worth remembering that the subsequent conjuror
with the willow laid for himself the foundation of solid
defence before, confident in this strength, he began to execute
those strokes which for many years have been the delight
and despair of fellow cricketers. In his most brilliant period
no one knew better than Victor Trumper the risks his
magical strokes involved.

When Victor Trumper hit his brilliant century at Lord's in
1899 (of which match more in Chapter Ten), it led to a letter
and a newspaper cutting on 19 June 1899 from H. Haigh
Hartley, who ran an Ancient and Modern Bookselling shop at
101 Park Street off Regent's Park, in London. It ran:

Dear Sir,
    In looking through my private cricket collection yesterday
I came across the enclosed leaf from the *Sporting Magazine*
of 1827 which records a remarkable exploit in the cricket
world by a namesake of yours. It may perhaps be of interest
to you; if so, I shall be pleased if you would accept it from
me as some little memento of the pleasure I had in witness-
ing your fine batting in the Test match at Lord's last week.
                        I am, yours faithfully,
                        H. H. Hartley.

I have the letter and the cutting, loaned to me by Mrs Syd
Trumper. They are now yellow with age but the cutting is also

worth quoting. Under the title of 'Cricket' – sub-titled a 'novel game of cricket' – it runs:

A novel game of cricket was played on Monday, 21st May, on Harefield Common, for a considerable sum, between two gentlemen of Middlesex and Mr Francis Trumper, farmer at Harefield, with the help of a thoroughbred sheep dog. In the first innings, the two gentlemen got three runs, and Mr Trumper three for himself and two for his dog. In the second innings, the two gentlemen again got three runs and Mr Trumper, then going in and getting two runs, beat the two gentlemen, having got two wickets standing. Before the game began the odds were 5-1 against Mr Trumper and his canine partner; but after the first innings the situation was so altered that bets of 4-1 on were laid on Trumper and his dog. The match being much talked about in the neighbourhood for two or three weeks and the day proving fine, there was a numerous attendance of spectators, who were much astonished at the dog's dexterity. The dog always stood near his master when he was going to bowl; and the moment the ball was hit he kept his eye upon the ball and started off after it with speed; and on his master running up to the wicket the dog would carry the ball in his mouth, and put it into his master's hand so quickly that the gentlemen found it very difficult to get a run even from the longest hit. The money lost and won on the occasion was considerable, as a great number of gentlemen came from Uxbridge and the neighbouring towns and villages to see so extraordinary a game.

This may well have been the first printed mention of the name of Trumper in cricket.

4

A Fluke Trip to England

How Trumper ever got to England in 1899 was a miracle, and a tribute to his fellows and especially those New South Welshmen who had such faith in him. For his entry into first-class cricket was hardly illustrious.

For instance, in January 1895 he played for NSW against South Australia at Adelaide and was run out in the first innings for eleven. Elliott Monfries, who kept wicket for Victoria, tells in his chatty little book *Not Test Cricket* how Trumper pulled George Giffen's leg in that game, the first time he had played against him. Giffen at that time was a 'big gun' in Australian cricket, a great batsman, a great bowler and a cricketer with a very safe pair of hands. He captained the South Australian side for years and gave followers of the game the impression that only one man should be bowling or batting, and that man was Giffen. Even after playing a long innings under a wickedly hot sun George would start the bowling and also end it, notwithstanding many shrill and insistent calls from the clientele round the fence to 'take yourself off, George.' So absolutely impervious was he to such gentle advice that the home supporters would resort to satire and loudly advise him to put on the local groundsman, Charlie Checkett. Satire would sometimes be followed by abuse and perhaps at long last Giffen would throw the ball to another bowler to the accompaniment of uproarious applause. Upon the new bowler finishing his over imagine the chagrin and utter disgust of George's numerous friends when he took up the attack at the other end: bedlam!

Trumper, still a lithe, narrow-shouldered schoolboy, could not resist pulling George's leg. Giffen used to make many caught and bowleds, concealing his pace, hanging the ball back and then, running down the pitch, make the catch from a dolly stroke by the confused batsman. He tried this with Trumper and the new boy caused much amusement when, picking the intention of it, he just coolly popped the ball over George's head. Had Giffen stood his ground he would have had a simple catch. George used to grin when he got a batsman out like this but they said there wasn't a glimmer of a smile when Trumper, in his first Sheffield Shield innings and against one of the Australian giants of the game, outwitted him.

It was Giffen who did the smiling in the second innings when Ernie Jones caught Trumper off Giffen's bowling for a duck. Trumper was to make an inordinate number of ducks in his career, but even with only eleven runs in this match Adelaide men who knew the game thought that Trumper showed great promise and should have been retained by NSW. He came into the side against Queensland but did little worth noting, making six and five not out. Then he was chosen for NSW against Stoddart's second team in 1897 and in the first innings was caught by Ranjitsinhji off Hirst for five and clean bowled by Tom Richardson in the second innings for a duck.

If there was nothing glittering in those performances to justify the critics going to town about Trumper, Noble at least remembered Trumper's début for a catch off Hayward which he felt was probably the most sensational and spectacular he had ever seen in the outfield.

Hayward hit a ball, which I bowled, and he hit it long and low over mid-off's head. Calculating where it would land, Victor dashed in at top speed, made a baseball dive at the ball, caught it, turned a complete somersault, and finished on his back, with the ball in one hand, held high in the air. One sees few such catches in a lifetime.

From Noble's description it was the counterpart of a catch which Jeff Thomson took at Sydney, also in the outfield, when he caught Murray, the West Indian wicket-keeper, off Walker. That was the best catch I have seen. Thomson said on a television show when I interviewed him that he was angered at Greg Chappell taking him off and when he saw Murray hit the ball high he decided that he just had to catch it!

Noble himself, incidentally, I once saw at Waverley take a first-slip catch that came to him like lightning and then, almost without catching it, transfer it to the man at second slip – a lovely piece of playing to the gallery.

Noble, who in his time wrote splendidly on cricket and told amusing anecdotes on the game, relates how cricket in NSW during the 1890s was languishing under a spell of orthodoxy and passive resistance and was fast throttling the people's appreciation of the game and destroying the allegiance of many of its supporters. 'Victor's wonderful demonstrations shocked old ideas and brought light out of semi-darkness. With his coming the old order passed for ever.'

Noble also relates how in the Sydney club season of 1898–9 a very handsome shield was offered to the highest aggregate in club cricket. Towards the end of the season Trumper was well behind and needed almost 200 runs in his last innings to have a chance. When he left his Paddington home on the morning of the last match he said to his mother: 'I'm going to get you that shield today,' and he did, making 253.

However, there were many at this time who shook their heads and said of the young Trumper: 'He is too flash. He cannot last. His methods are not those of a great batsman.' And for a while it seemed the critics were right. After the Adelaide match – and the encounter with Giffen – Trumper was left out of the State team for the next two years. He caused tongues to wag, however, on 7 and 9 November 1896, when he made 113 not out for the next XV against NSW on the SCG. That same year Noble induced him to join Paddington, of which club Noble was captain. Trumper was 19 years old. Noble knew the great batsman he had in the making and wanted to have his former fellow pupil under his guidance, knowing also that the South Sydney club would be sunk by electorate club cricket. In Paddington, too, he would be with class players and be batting first on a first-class pitch, good enough for a Test match (when dear old Paddy Ryan was curator).

Trumper had already shown his class in other matches before joining Paddington. In December 1894 he was one of 15 Colts of NSW who played against A. E. Stoddart's first team, a type of game which sadly has fallen into desuetude in both England and Australia, and on the morning of the match he was running a temperature from 'flu. His mother did not want him to go to the cricket ground, but Victor was persistent and, in company with a sister, went there and scored 67 against bowling from proven Test stars like Lockwood and Peel. The only person not impressed was Mrs Trumper, who promptly on his return put her son to bed and ordered him to stay there.

Within a year Trumper's class told. In 1897 his scores ran:

North Sydney	run out	82
Central Cumberland	c. Donoghue, b. Howell	123
South Sydney (his old club)	b. Connell	125
Waverley	c. M'Intyre, b. Noonan	85
Glebe	not out	120
Burwood	not out	191
Redfern	b. Creswick	133
Leichhardt	not out	162

Noble notes that Trumper's average was 204·20. Noble's own average, next season, when he was only twice out, was 273. Don Bradman, feeling his way, so to speak, in Sydney cricket in 1929–30 averaged 109, the next year averaged 170, the year after that 112. It is interesting that Geoff Boycott, in the season 1976–7, when he was playing with Waverley, averaged 165·71. Boycott simply did not get enough not-outs. Thus Noble's average has never been beaten.

One final point about that Stoddart match of Trumper's. In his book on that tour Ranjitsinhji wrote:

Trumper created a very favourable impression on me from the way in which he was shaping at the wickets. He seemed to be all there and the confidence with which he played the bowling, although it was for a very short time, made me firmly believe that he will be a very great batsman in this country and at no very distant date.

This was a remarkable prophecy, written, as it was, in 1898 of an innings of only five, and with all Trumper's great innings still to come.

Noble saw all these outstanding club innings by Trumper and it was but natural that he should favour his choice for the tour of England in 1899. But the fact remained that, in his few brief appearances for NSW, Trumper had been a failure.

Hughie Trumble of Melbourne, Syd Gregory of Sydney, and Joe Darling, then of South Australia and also the Australian captain, were the selectors. Gregory thought like Noble – he wanted Trumper in the party. But Victoria and South Australia were just as strongly against Trumper, for they argued – with justification, as Noble was forced to admit – 'We have good young cricketers with figures to support them. We have not seen your Trumper.' That, said Noble, was just the trouble, and what the New South Welshmen were telling those from other States: 'You haven't seen Trumper in full flight. Once you do there will be no doubt in your minds, as there is no doubt in ours.'

To Noble's infinite disgust he was the unwilling instrument of Trumper's dismissal in two of the three trial matches. He had pertinent thoughts when Trumper hit back a catch, not an easy one, when he'd scored 26 in Melbourne. The temptation came into Noble's mind, 'Miss it, miss it,' but he didn't and he thought his disappointment even greater than Trumper's because the young batsman was then moving into top gear.

Noble used to argue strongly with Hugh Trumble when he met him in Melbourne or Sydney. Those who are certain of their own place in a touring team never hesitate to express their thoughts on other players to those who are in a selecting position. True, their views are often sought. Sometimes a mate can be given good support; but it can work the other way too,

E

as a star can work off a dislike for a particular individual. 'Hughie,' said Noble once to Trumble in Melbourne, 'you know me. I wouldn't give you a bum steer. I've seen young Trumper in Sydney this summer play club innings that are out of this world. He would be the talk of England. They have not seen anybody like him before.' Trumble stroked his chin. 'Yes, Monty, I believe you. But why hasn't young Trumper done this in some first-class matches? It is pretty difficult when he fails time after time when others succeed. We can only go on what we see, can't we?'

Oddly, Noble thought that it was a Victorian, J. M'Lauchlin, a vice-president of the Melbourne Cricket Club, who changed Victorian minds about Trumper. He travelled to Sydney to see the Trial match and there saw Trumper play one of his master-pieces of an innings for Paddington – 260 not out. M'Lauchlin knew genius when he saw it, and went back to Melbourne and spread the gospel. But it was too late. The team was announced, and Trumper was not in it. To Noble the exclusion was incomprehensible, but luckily, before the team sailed for England, it was decided they should play three matches against the Rest of Australia, one each in Sydney, Melbourne and Adelaide. Joe Darling says in his son's book (*Test Tussles on and off the Field* by D. K. Darling) that Trumper played in all three.

He did only fairly in Sydney and Melbourne and did not impress either Trumble or myself as a coming champion. Yet in the match in Adelaide he played a superb innings of 75 against the Australian Eleven. Trumble and I were then convinced that Trumper was a coming champion and we realized we had made a mistake in not selecting him, owing to the chance we had never seen him at his best.

Wardill, manager of the side, came over to Noble in Adelaide and asked: 'You want Trumper in this side?' 'Rather,' said Noble. 'Then go to him and tell him he is going. We are taking an extra man.' Trumper was to go at a reduced fee, and one of his jobs was to assist the manager – probably lending a hand with the laundry, organizing the autographs and letters and running messages.

The *Sydney Morning Herald* of 23 March 1899 commented:

It was hinted a few days ago in this column that Trumper would probably go to England in different terms from the rest of the team. It now transpires on good authority that he proceeds there as an amateur, that his expenses will be paid and he will receive a bonus of £200 as far as the English tour is concerned. Should the team visit America, New Zealand, or Tasmania, he will share alike in the matches played in those countries. Should he be a success in England the agreement provides that his claims to a larger bonus or an equal share in the profits of the tour will be considered.

Ray Robinson, in his outstanding book *On Top Down Under*, says that the bonus for the 1899 players was about £700, good money in those days. I doubt, however, whether any union in Australia would allow one of its members to go on a tour at terms disadvantageous to the others. One for all, all for one. And anyway, after the Lord's Test, his fellows had no compunction in raising him to full bonus and full status. More immediately important, he had made the trip: Victor Trumper was going to England.

5

The First English Tour

Trumper had a woeful start to his first English tour. He was clean bowled by Young of Essex at Leyton for nil. Young also clean bowled him in the second innings for three and the prominent professional, Tom Hayward, clean bowled him at the Oval against Surrey for 13. He was run out for 13 against an English eleven at Eastbourne but showed glimpses of his true form in the second innings with 62. In the next match against Lancashire, at Old Trafford, he made 82 before he was again clean bowled.

Like most Australians on their first tour of England, he was slow to come to grips with the varying turf. (The brilliant Bradman was a notable exception, making 236 in 1930 in his first innings at Worcester.) Even ordinary bowlers can seam and cut the ball off most English pitches, and it was interesting that Trumper should have been clean bowled in five of his first seven innings in England. The words of Trumper's early critics in Australia recurred to many Australian minds that he was too flash, too prone to leave himself and his wicket open. His first Test at Trent Bridge was a disaster. Jack Hearne sent his stumps wheeling in the first innings for yet another duck and Jackson clean bowled him for 29 when the Australians played MCC at Lord's, so that young Trumper, who batted six and five at Trent Bridge, had done little up to the time of the second Test at Lord's. Then, amazingly, he hit his straps with a vengeance, his 135 not out, again at number six, setting the English cricket world agog. It was Trumper at his undoubted best, and Englishmen marvelled at the brilliancy of his stroke-play. He played, said one critic, 'with astonishing grace and freedom for a young man only in his second Test'.

Newspapers today would have featured to the minutest degree the family, career and background of anybody who made such a brilliant entry into Test cricket and at Lord's, of all places, but the newspapers of that time give very little detail in analysing such scores. *The Times* was very perfunctory in its reports, talking about the weather and giving little detail of the play. It also called all the Australian cricketers 'Mr'. A lot of Englishmen resented the fuss, standing and attention given the Colonials, some of whom had very lowly positions at home – Gregory, for instance, being an assistant on the Sydney Cricket Ground staff.

I think the scene as Trumper returned to the pavilion must have resembled that which Greg Chappell knew in 1972 when the whole ground rose to him after his classic century innings of 131.

The *Sydney Morning Herald* of that time always made the tour its main cable story and the main heading was always the same: 'Australian Cricketers'. It is interesting to reflect how the *Herald* covered the tour. Perhaps they seconded a member of their main London staff while the real cricket expert added comments from Sydney. Against Sussex the story merited a whole glut of headlines:

The Australian Cricketers
The Match against Sussex
Four Wickets for 624
Innings Declared Closed
Brilliant Batting by Trumper
He Scores 300 Not Out
The Match Drawn

They were exceptional headlines for the period. Vying for space in the cables were Captain Dreyfus, the alleged French spy, and the fact that troops and arms were being hurried to South Africa. On 3 July, for instance, Captain Dreyfus met his wife at Rennes. It was reported that the captain, who, seemingly, had been put to torture to extract 'confessions', was dazed and inarticulate. 'The interview on both sides was one long sob,' said the cable.

A little similar ingenuity might have been used on the

Sussex match. One wonders why the sub on the desk, realizing from his own headlines that he had something most unusual, did not write an introduction to the story something like: 'The young NSW batsman, Victor Trumper, today against Sussex at Brighton, became the first Australian batsman in cricket history to hit 300 in England. He was not out when Darling declared. Trumper played a scintillating innings, his strokes being most powerful and in all directions. His innings was chanceless to 300 when he was badly dropped at mid-off.' But there was nothing.

The *Herald* man on the job in England was not very expansive in his cables. He contented himself by writing the scores, a habit some journalists still persist in, despite the fact that they have been sent enormous distances at great cost to give a 'specialized' report of the tour. On Monday 24 July, for instance, the *Herald* man cabled:

> On resumption of play after lunch, the Australians opened their innings by sending in Laver and Iredale. The former scored eight and then was bowled by Martin. Trumper followed and when the total had reached 27 Iredale was 12 and Trumper six. With 42 runs added Trumper was bowled by Grace for 25. Two for 67, Iredale 30. The vacancy was filled by Gregory who scored freely and faster than his partner. When the total was raised to nearly 150 the partnership was broken, Gregory being caught by Champain off Foster for 48, Iredale having augmented his score to over 50. Darling succeeded and when he had obtained 22 – the total being over 180 – he was caught by Grace off Winter. Just before the call of time, Noble went in, got a single, and then stumps were drawn.

There is nothing very illuminating in that, but some five weeks after it was written the *Herald* carried a long article from 'A Special Correspondent', whom I surmise to have been F. S. Ashley-Cooper, a noted English cricket correspondent, which gave more comments on the tour. When Lockwood took

7–71 off 40.3 overs in the fifth Test at the Oval that year the *Herald* in Sydney commented that Mr Ashley-Cooper had offered the opinion in a letter at the opening of the season – 'and he is a recognized cricket authority' – that Lockwood's bowling would come as a surprise to the Australians and that he was probably the best all-rounder in England. But he suffered from a strain all the summer and this was the only Test for which he was fit, though he broke down again in the second innings.

The Australians went from Birmingham down to Truro in Cornwall and, being most unusual visitors there, they were entertained by the Cornish people in great style. Mr Ashley-Cooper noted that the ground was a beautiful one but it was set on a hill and sloped away on three sides, while one boundary was so low that only the top of the far wicket could be seen from the outfield. 'Here,' said the special correspondent – and it is interesting that they suffered in those days similar difficulties to those we have now – 'I must break off to catch the mail, a further account of the Birmingham match which I sent up to town three days ago having in some unaccountable way gone missing in the post.' One presumes 'town' was London and that the letter was then sent on to Australia by mail steamer.

Trumper required 21 to get his thousand for the tour against Sussex but before the Australians batted, Sussex, thanks mainly to Fry, had indulged in a run orgy. The *Herald* man cabled very accurately as it proved: 'The match between the Australians and Sussex was resumed at Brighton today. The weather is lovely and the wicket good. The attendance numbered 4000. The home team, which had lost six wickets for 389 at the conclusion of the previous day's play, resumed its innings. The bowlers can't get much "work" on the ball and they therefore expect to be knocked about.' They were. Charles Fry got a splendid 181, batting for four hours and hitting 25 fours. Ranjitsinhji was bowled by M'Leod for six and at one stage Fry was 105 not out, out of 2–154. He got a tremendous ovation when his innings finished, caught Trumble off M'Leod.

Hill, who had just recently had a growth cut out of his nose in London, collapsed after the gruelling run-chasing and had to retire.

Sussex were all out for 414. The reporter was induced to write about record scores at that time. The highest was Yorkshire's 887 against Warwickshire in 1896, and then came Australia's 813 against the Past and Present of Oxford and Cambridge in 1893 and then, a few weeks before this game at Sussex, Surrey's 811 against my 'home' county, Somerset. (It is of interest in these cigarette-sponsored days that the Non-Smokers made 103 against the Smokers at the Melbourne Cricket Ground in 1887. I wonder if such a game would be sponsored today?) Somerset were again on the receiving end in 1895 when Lancashire made 801 against them at Taunton.

The *Herald*, near the bottom of its column, said Trumper topped 160, the previous highest score for the tour made by Clem Hill.

> He did not give a chance and his driving and pulling were excellent. Trumper and Gregory played with great dash and runs came apace. Trumper had long since passed his second century. Various bowling changes were resorted to but without effect. Trumper hit all round and punished the bowlers with vigour. He treated all bowlers alike, being particularly strong on the pull and the drive. 600 appeared on the board and soon afterwards Trumper reached his third century. Trumper batted in slashing style all through his innings, which lasted six-and-a-quarter hours, and never gave a chance until reaching his third century when he was badly missed at mid-off.

That innings by Trumper against Sussex had very much sapped him. His skipper, Joe Darling, said he was worn out for some weeks and Joe, deciding to conserve his strength, rarely used Trumper as a bowler (and he was still a very fair medium to fast bowler who could break partnerships). After his 300 not out Trumper made 4, 0, 9 not out, 50, 13, 6, 7, 1 and 2. But all were agreed, after his 135 in his first Test (his first first-class

1. A portrait study of Trumper taken in Melbourne in 1902.

2. Reg Duff (left) and Trumper, the legendary opening pair, come out to start Australia's innings in the third Test at Adelaide, 1903-4. Duff, in making 79, for once out-shone Trumper in a first wicket stand of 129. Trumper then went on to score 113, his third century in five Tests.

3. The Australian team that toured England in 1899. Trumper, on the extreme left, and added to the party at the last moment, has not yet been awarded the Australian blazer. *Standing:* V. Trumper, H. Trumble, A. E. Johns, W. P. Howell, Maj. Wardill, M. A. Noble, F. Laver, C. E. McLeod. *Seated:* J. J. Kelly, C. Hill, J. Worrall, J. J. Darling, F. A. Iredale, E. Jones. *On ground:* S. E. Gregory.

. The best-known of all photographs of Trumper.

. The follow-through.

6. In 1905 the Australians came to England via New Zealand, Fiji and Canada. While in NZ they went boating on the Whangunai River, taking pot shots at pigeons, ducks, birds and pigs (final score: nil). Warwick Armstrong is aiming the rifle. Trumper is behind him, with 'Dutch' cap pulled over his eyes. Pointing the way is Monty Noble.

7. Trumper in goat-drawn carriage — one of the few photographs that remain showing him in informal mood. It was taken at Hastings during the 1905 tour.

century, incidentally, after his 292 not out against Tasmania for NSW in 1898. Two earlier centuries, against Queensland and even New Zealand, were not deemed first class), that a batsman out of the ordinary had been discovered. He was in addition a superlative fieldsman, fast and safe. With a slight run he could throw 115 yards, and his returns to the wicket were said not to waste time in gaining elevation: they came in fast and low. He owed this, he said, to playing baseball in the winter.

Charles Fry got 10 in the second innings and Ranjitsinhji 15, both falling to Ernie Jones. There was some light comedy in Sussex's second innings when Joe Darling gave Clem Hill a bowl. Clem was no bowler but he so studiously set his field and took so long over it that Darling warned him if he didn't get on with the game somebody else would get a bowl. So Clem got on with it and clean bowled Killick, middle stump, much to everybody's delight apart from Killick's but particularly so to Clem Hill's. He promptly turned somersaults on the field and was converged on by his fellows who pumped his hand in excitement and surprise. Clem was a very popular cricketer with his fellows and was always up to practical jokes.

Trumper made a typical gesture at the end of the Sussex game. The players had two long cricket bags each and carried their spare gear in the second one. Joe Darling did not have cause to open his second bag for several weeks after the game. When he did so he found in it Trumper's bat. It was inscribed: 'To Joe Darling, with Victor Trumper's compliments.' It was, of course, the bat with which Trumper had made his historic 300 not out.

Trumper was to make his second century of the tour, 104, against Gloucestershire down at Bristol, but most meritorious was his second innings in the fourth Test at Old Trafford. Bradley, of Kent, had taken the place of Briggs, who, in the previous Test, had suffered a fit while at the theatre one evening during the match. Hayward hit perhaps his greatest century at Old Trafford and it was interesting that F. S. Jackson should have been caught off a bouncer from Jones. Noble, who had made a 'pair' at Headingley, this time made 60 not out

out of 196 and the Australians, forced to follow on, saw Noble bat eight-and-a-half hours for 89. They also realized they had struck a troublesome wicket, and Trumper, going in fourth, batted brilliantly for 63.

There was one other, interesting feature of that tour. Sent at several hours' intervals, the *Herald*'s cables told of the brilliant progress towards a century of a batsman named Champain, who was captain of Oxford. One cable sent at 2.20 p.m. said Champain, batting in splendid style, had increased his score to 106. Later he had gone to 120 in the same faultless style, and his name appears in later matches as catching some Australians out. But whatever happened to one who batted so brilliantly and who greatly aided Oxford to head the Australians in their first innings, 341 to 302?

The *Herald* man also wrote in high praise of Trumper's innings at Lord's: 'It is impossible to give Trumper too much praise for his magnificent score. He made it without a blemish. His was by far the most attractive batting of the match and his success is very popular with other members of his side. His splendid conduct has in every way endeared him to his comrades off the field as well as his splendid play on it.'

Overall it was a wet, miserably cold summer, a summer in which the Australians suffered frequently from colds and influenza. Darling said that it was so cold at Lord's once that some of the team wore their blazers underneath their flannel shirts to keep out the cold. Often Australians in England have left a blazing fire in their dressing-room to go to the middle to bat, clad in two or three sweaters. How they fielded at Lord's with a blazer added to their clothing challenges the imagination, but Darling declares this was so.

In all Trumper scored eleven centuries that tour, his highest being 128 against Cambridge. He also made 121 against Oxford. Trumper enjoyed playing against the Universities. He liked the atmosphere of mixing with the undergraduates and being in places of learning. In addition to his eleven centuries he made 92 against Gloucestershire and 96 against the Players in the final match of the tour at the Oval, Rhodes catching and bowling him – so he came within a whisper of 13 centuries on a tour.

He also made 86 in the second innings against MCC and Staff at Lord's, after his century, so that he very nearly performed earlier the feat of a century in each innings which he was to do later against Essex at Leyton.

It was obvious that many innings by Trumper that season were played on 'sticky' pitches. I turn to that shrewd old cricketing head of Hughie Trumble for his opinions on pitches in both England and Australia when affected by rain. In the Melbourne *Sun-News Pictorial* in May 1927 he wrote:

There is a lack of knowledge among recognized players concerning the various conditions of pitches affected by rain. It is quite a common occurrence after inspection of a pitch to find half the side wanting to put the opposition in if they won the toss and the other half wanting to bat. In England it doesn't always follow that a soft pitch is going to be particularly bad. I recall an incident in the 'nineties when an Australian captain [Blackham], after winning the toss at Lord's in a match against MCC and Staff, put the other side in. It had been raining steadily for a couple of days prior to the match and the ground was saturated. Small scores seemed the order of the day, but the move turned out disastrously. In the absence of wind or sun the pitch played slow and easy without any life or bite, and the members of our team were shocked when over 400 runs were scored by five o'clock, two of the Englishmen making centuries. Our skipper was so upset that he declared that if he lived to be as old as Methuselah he would never again put the other side in in England.

There is a good deal of difference between wickets in Australia and England after rain. In Australia it would be impossible to get a pitch to play at all easily for any great length of time after rain, whether it was affected by the sun or not. On some grounds in England it is possible for a wicket to dry naturally and slowly after a good soaking and never get really difficult. Of course, the 'sticky' pitch gives the bowler his day out but it is not every bowler who can take advantage of it. Bowlers, as a rule, do not keep the ball up

enough on these wickets, and what may be a fair length ball
on a fast pitch is much too short for a slow-paced one and
may be easily pulled to leg. A bowler cannot afford to bowl
any bad length balls on a sticky pitch when forcing batsmen
are about and looking for runs all the time. A good left-
hander is invaluable on English pitches. It does not always
follow if a pitch is wet it is going to be difficult, especially
in England where the soil is not of that sticky nature so
common in Australia. In Australia the grass, mostly couch,
is shaved right down to the roots; but this practice is not
adopted in England. The grass there is not so closely cut and
seldom loses its natural colour. The pitches there receive
nothing like the preparation they get in Australia and play
a good deal slower, which gives the batsman more time to
watch the ball. In an English summer one gets every type
of pitch to bowl on with the easy, slow one predominating,
that is the pitch affected by rain but allowed to dry naturally
without the sun's rays as a rule. Recalling the summer of
1902, which was a particularly wet one, some members of
our team said they had not seen the sun for three weeks in
mid-summer – or mid-winter, as some declared they thought
it was. Wet weather has a disheartening effect on players
and spectators alike. It is no uncommon thing in England to
see thousands of spectators at a Test, or other good match,
braving the elements and squatting around in the rain the
best part of a day, hoping for a start. They naturally think
that if they can brave the rain the players can too. The
test in W.G.'s day, when he led the side, was: 'Are the
umbrellas down yet? We are not going out until they are,'
and he didn't. The only time I saw him forced out against
his will was in a Test at the Oval. The county committee
was in a dilemma as the crowd of some 20,000 had been
waiting in the rain most of the day and looked like getting
out of hand. The committee begged the captains to make a
start and pacify the public. Water was lying on the pitch
and it was palpably unfit for play. However, W.G. won the
toss and the game went on. The bowlers could not get a
footing and the ball was like a lump of grease. The batsmen

had it all their own way and the 60-odd runs they got in
that hour practically won the game for England.

A batsman of intelligence and resource should very soon
adapt himself to the altered conditions of English pitches.
A batsman who has grit and can punch an over-pitched ball
and develop his footwork and back-play should be quite able
to hold his own even if the season is wet. The trouble with
most batsmen is that they seem to lose heart when the pitch
is affected by rain.

Trumper filled all those requirements of what a batsman
should possess in heart and mind in 1902. Joe Darling, his
skipper, lamented the fact that Trumper inherited a weak constitution, which, he says, eventually led to his death, and Joe
tells of how he had to nurse Trumper along. 'Unfortunately,
owing to the fact that he did not enjoy the best of health,
Trumper had many bad days, but when fit and well there was
only one cricketer in it as champion of the world, and that was
Trumper,' wrote Joe in his memoirs.

I find much of interest in what E. H. D. Sewell wrote of
Trumper in his *Cricket Under Fire*. He says that Trumper was
one of those players to whom there seemed no such thing as
a good-length ball. Every ball bowled to him became the
'Trumper length' ball. 'I claim some right to be assertive on this
point,' adds Sewell, 'as I fielded in the only first-class match in
which Trumper made a century in each innings. And what's
the good of having a front seat when Genius is in action if you
do not see and learn something? I also had the honour of being
bowled by him. He bowled medium-fast, about Tate's pace.'

Sewell wrote that he thought Trumper could have made
stacks and stacks more runs than he did. 'I should guess that
his proportion of scores between 100 and 120 is of all those
of the Great Ones easily the highest. He was never, like Bradman and Ponsford, runs-greedy.' It has often been said that the
best Australian batsmen, after they had made their hundred,
just settle down with a 'Now for the second one.' Assuredly,
that was untrue of Trumper and Macartney. Nobody ever got
just a little bored while they were at the wicket – always with

the exception of a blunt Notts miner who, asked what he thought of Charlie Macartney's 345 at Trent Bridge in 1921, all of it in one day, replied promptly: 'Bloody monotonous.'

Success on that 1902 tour never went to Trumper's head. In his book *Cricket is My Life* Len Hutton tells a story of Trumper that is legendary in Yorkshire, where they appreciate such generous qualities. Trumper had carved the best Yorkshire bowlers to bits and a young collier, who had gained his county place after good club feats, was given the ball. He was understandably anxious and nervous and it was reasonable that he could not find his length at all. Did Trumper murder him? Not in the slightest. He made no attempt whatsoever to score off the young man's bowling. He admitted afterwards that he didn't want to 'spoil that lad's chance of getting a living in an easier way than heaving coal'.

There was a similar case in the match against Lancashire when the Australians played them at Liverpool. In the Lancashire team was a young bowler named Kermode who had travelled from Australia to try to make his way in English cricket. Trumper knew that he was having a hard time of it and would be lucky to keep his place in the Lancashire team. When he came on to bowl Trumper gave Kermode the greatest respect and was finally bowled by him for six. Nobody said it but many thought Trumper gave him his wicket to help him along the way. Kermode was later to return to Australia and play with the Sydney club, Balmain.

Clem Hill told of the spirit of the game that permeated cricket in those days, unlike the so-called 'sledging' of today when players deliberately set out to bait the opposition by niggling at them. George Robey, the famous English comedian, would come down to Lord's and practise with the Australians, and Trumper's hardest job in the nets was to miss a straight one: Robey didn't send many such down. The tourists of those days were inveterate attenders at the London music halls, and Clem told of the day at Lord's when, while they were waiting for the next batsman to come in, six of the Australians gathered in the middle of Lord's and sang a song then popular in the music halls.

Clem quoted MacLaren as saying he envied the Australians
the way they could relax and then gather all their faculties
together when they were needed. And indeed nerves must have
been the order of the day at Old Trafford in a Test which
Australia won by three runs and which was the greatest Test
played up to that time and, apart from the tied Test in Brisbane
against the West Indians, the greatest ever. I have read much
of this earlier Test, and it has always seemed to me that Fred
Tate, the father of Maurice, was unfairly made the scapegoat
for England's defeat. England left out Fry and Jessop, restored
Ranjitsinhji to the place he had been unable to take at Sheffield,
and brought in Palairet and Tate. The editor of *Wisden* said he
agreed with the dropping of Fry, as he had failed in three Tests,
but he said it was a mistake not to play Jessop, who would have
strengthened the fielding on the off-side. Neville Cardus, who
proudly claimed that as a schoolboy sitting under the ropes he
had his shins bruised by a drive from Trumper in that game,
wrote a most colourful story of this Test in which he also made
Tate out to be the main offender. That was more than hard on
Tate. England, after a game of amazing fluctuations, had
Australia three down for ten in the second innings and, sensing
an English kill, the atmosphere was fiercely partisan. In all the
stir Tate missed Joe Darling on the square-leg boundary when
the score was still only sixteen. Darling and Gregory then took
the score to 64.

With Australia all out for 86 in the second innings England
wanted only 123 to win. It rained during the second night, and
it was some time before play began on the final day; but
England were well on the road to victory, having scored 36
without loss, and with Palairet and MacLaren in control.

On resuming after lunch Saunders clean bowled Palairet.
Johnny Tyldesley was in his home county and before his own
people and the Australians knew well Tyldesley's capabilities.
He got a start too – he had reached sixteen – but then Armstrong took him in the slips, again off Saunders. That made it
68–2 with only 56 wanted, and with MacLaren batting well.
He was the pride of Lancashire and the whole ground wanted
him to be in at the death. Then he fell to a beautiful running

catch by Duff in the deep and at 72–3 the Australians wondered whether they now had a chance.

They had. Ranjitsinhji was a mass of nerves in the dressing-room – so much so that some of the Australians there said he had gone so pale that MacLaren even thought of putting him in last. Hill said he had never seen the Indian prince bat so badly. 'One would have thought he was on the worst wicket it was possible to produce,' said Hill. He goes on:

He poked about like a novice and not even Ranji was surprised when he was LBW to Trumble. 92 for four. England wanted only 32 and had six wickets in hand. Our fighting blood was up and the wicket had become sticky. We were on our toes. How we fielded! And how Trumble and Saunders bowled!

Abel had made nearly all the runs while Ranji was in, but then Trumble bowled him neck and crop. Five down for 97. Then Jackson, the hero of the first innings, tried to place a full-toss from Saunders between mid-off and cover and little Syd Gregory, leaping high into the air, brought off a wonderful catch.

Still another 17 wanted and four more wickets to fall. The excitement was intense. Jones and Howell, who were in the stand, told us afterwards that they felt the suspense terribly. Men leaned forward in their seats, watching every ball and cheering every run.

Braund was stumped off Trumble with two more runs added and the tall Victorian then bowled the great bowler, Lockwood, without any addition to the score. Eight for 109. Another 15 were wanted when Rhodes and Lilley came together. Singles took the score to 116.

Then Lilley had a hit, tempting death or glory. The ball went skimming between long-on and square-leg towards me. I raced after it with not the slightest intention of a catch but with the determination to save a boundary. Almost on the boundary, after running the best part of 25 yards, I threw everything to chance and made a dive for the ball. Nobody was more astonished than I to find the ball had stuck. I could hardly realize I had made the catch. I was the proudest man on the ground. Poor Lilley, passing me on the way in, called out: 'Oh, Clem, what a bally fluke.' I had to reply, 'Never on your life, Dick,' but he knew the truth and so did I. Nine for 116.

Tate was next. His feelings, sitting in the dressing-room with the pads on, can easily be imagined. He had just reached the middle when down came the rain and the players ran from the field. Hill says there was a 30-minute stay in the dressing-room, and during that time the Australians thought that the English would get the runs. They had a greasy ball now with which to bowl, but as Rhodes looked like getting the runs on his own they determined not only to keep him from scoring but to prevent him getting to the other end off the last ball of the over.

How Old Trafford must have hummed during those 30 minutes! When they got out again Trumble very carefully arranged his field, adding to Tate's and Rhodes's worries and impressing the situation on them. When Tate faced Saunders England wanted only eight. The first ball grazed Tate's stumps (Rhodes having successfully been kept away from the strike). The second was snicked by Tate down to fine-leg. Armstrong, not then the huge, bulky man he was to become, raced as he had never done before or since to cut off the four. Luckily for Australia the ball beat him, or otherwise the more redoubtable batsman, Rhodes, would have faced Saunders. Tate faced up again and Saunders bowled him a 'trimmer' that knocked his off stump out of the ground. Hill said he had a vision for days afterwards of turf clinging to the end of the uprooted stump and the second bail still poised on the other two stumps. Darling said he had a constant nightmare that night of an off-stump being sent a-wheeling. It was certainly a great match, but it only brought sorrow for poor Tate. He sought the seclusion of a hansom-cab, in which he drew the blinds, and set off for the station. His only companion was his son, Maurice, who was to redeem the family's cricket name years later. Maurice said his father was crying.

F

I can well understand how he felt; yet years later I feel some recompense should be made to his memory. His dropped catch stuck in Englishmen's gullets, but in getting nine for once out he excelled Ranji who got only two and four, and Tate, after 0–44 in the first innings, got 2–7 in the second. Fry, who seemed to know a lot of what went on behind the scenes, said MacLaren chose Tate in preference to Hirst out of pique with Lord Hawke, who had refused to make Schofield Haigh available. But all said and done, Tate was having a great season in 1902 and later had the final compensation of getting Trumper's wicket for the South of England for six at Bournemouth. And, in the final analysis, it was Trumper's century before lunch that really won the Test for Australia at Old Trafford.

It was a great Test series. England had Australia badly on the run at Edgbaston, in which the weather saved Australia, for rain washed out the second Test at Lord's. Australia had a good win at Sheffield (where no Test has been played since and none will because soccer has taken over a famous cricket ground) by 143 runs; and Trumper played what all called a 'truly great' innings on a 'sticky', making 62 out of 80 in 50 minutes against such bowlers as Hirst, Braund, Barnes, Jackson and Rhodes. There was the narrow Test win at Old Trafford, and one almost equally as exciting at the Oval, England winning by one wicket after a grand innings by the hitter, Gilbert Jessop, who made 104, during the excitement of which a parson dropped dead.

Mention of that brings me to Trumper's only superstition. It concerned parsons; if Victor saw one when going out to bat he reckoned that the fates would be against him. 'I don't know what it is, but it upsets me to see one of those chaps when I am going in,' he would lament to those in the dressing-room. He must have seen few parsons in England in 1902.

6

How Trumper Skinned Redfern

While still in England the Australian side decided they would
not, as previously planned, make a full South African tour.
The decision was understandable, as South Africa was constantly in the news, there was considerable movement of troops
and arms there from Britain, and the Boer War had only ended
on 31 May that year. Nevertheless Darling's team stopped off
in South Africa on their way back home and played several
matches.

On a matting wicket at Pretoria, the capital, the Australians
played their first match against a Transvaal eleven that
contained seven international players. The Transvaalers set
Australia 442. Trumper opened and was immediately at home
on the mat. He had batted on the mat in his early days at
Moore Park, but this pitch was different in that the mat was set
on ant-bed soil, a better proposition for both bowlers and batsmen in that there was not the excessive bounce that comes
from a concrete pitch.

Trumper immediately hit seven fours on the fast outfield in
51 minutes before lunch. He lost his first partner, Reg Duff, at
78, Duff making 36, and there was poor support from his
fellows. Clem Hill made only three, Armstrong went for six,
Noble nine, Joe Darling 34, Hopkins eleven, Howell six,
Trumble fourteen, Carter sixteen and Saunders one. Australia
would have been in a mess but for Trumper. He had nine fours
in his first 50, fifteen fours in his century, completed in 90
minutes. Trumper's score, going in first, of 218 out of 392, with
his second hundred coming in 190 minutes, was remarkable,
and captivated the South Africans. He hit three sixes (it is
interesting that the South Africans played six for over the

fence at that time), 29 fours, five threes and fourteen twos.

Of the other main results the first Test, at Johannesburg, was drawn, very creditably to South Africa; the second resulted in an easy win for the Australians; and the third, in Cape Town, the Australians won by ten wickets. Trumper made 63 and 37, then 18 and 13, next 52 and 13 at Durban against a Natal XI, 49 and 19 against a similar team at Cape Town, and 70 and 38 not out in the final Test. But undoubtedly his 218 not out at Pretoria, though not in a first-class game, was the innings of the tour. The weather, as well as the bowlers, gave Trumper much worry. The *Star* says the play at Pretoria began in a 'grateful' breeze, whatever that may be, but the light later became bad, as it can do in Johannesburg. Thunder was heard and the wind got up. This caused the dust to blow inconveniently for the players and rain drove them towards the marquee, but they were soon back and Trumper hit out magnificently. The *Star* correspondent frequently commended Trumper for 'legging' the ball prettily, and a batsman never 'came in' – he 'succeeded' the outgoing man. The report concludes: 'Trumper's craftsmanship on the Berea ground at Pretoria will long be a memory to those of us who had the good fortune to witness it.' Both England and South Africa had been conquered.

Back in Australia Trumper was soon into his stride, and in his first innings hit 165 against South Australia in Adelaide. Then Giffen had him leg before, as he had had him out in Sydney, in the return match, for 45. In the second innings Trumper was caught Hugo bowled Jones for seven.

Giffen and Jones were two tremendous Australians. I mentioned earlier how Giffen thought he should always keep one end going as a bowler. He often did. When England toured in the 1894–5 season Giffen captained Australia in four of the five Tests, Blackham leading in the first but, through injuries, then standing down for Giffen to take over. In Sydney's fourth Test Harry Trott surprisingly opened the bowling – the new ball being used for slow leg-breaks! – but the move succeeded, as MacLaren was stumped almost immediately. Trott had 3–21 and Turner 3–18. There was nothing in those figures to suggest a bowling change, but Giffen whipped Trott off, took the ball himself, and took the English tail with 3–14.

Giffen bowled 343 overs in the series. Nearest to him was Turner, with 187 overs. He also had star bowlers in his side in Trumble, Albert Trott and Ernie Jones. But Giffen, who could be said to have given himself every chance, topped both the bowling and batting aggregates. Giffen must have been very much a law unto himself, the counterpart in Australian cricket of Dr W. G. Grace. He once refused to leave the wicket when given out 'hit wicket' against Victoria and argued so volubly that he 'wasn't going' that Blackham continued the game under protest. Giffen went on to make 85.

He had a tough cricket upbringing. His father made a rule that unless he gave a good performance on Saturday afternoon he would go to bed without dinner. Under such a threat perhaps it was not surprising that by the time he was 20 Giffen was South Australia's best all-rounder. As colonial matches were confined to NSW and Victoria, Giffen didn't get a chance until Shaw's English team stopped off in Adelaide in 1881, on their way to the eastern States. He then scored a sparkling 95 against them, was chosen in the first Test, and stayed in the team until 1896.

In that first Test at the Oval in 1882 Giffen played with no great distinction, scoring two and nil and not getting a bowl; but as this Test saw the beginning of the Ashes he thus became a cricket immortal. He did better against the Gentlemen, taking 8–49 and clean bowling Dr Grace. The good Doctor seemed not to like it and when Giffen was batting insisted that Giffen's bat was too wide and called for a gauge to measure it. It passed muster, but W.G. had greatly annoyed the Australians with his charge, and when the Doctor came to bat again Giffen returned the compliment, called for the gauge, and this time the Doctor's bat was found to be too wide.

Giffen's all-round prowess was best shown against Victoria. In 1891, for South Australia, he scored 237 and took 12 wickets. In nine years to 1894 against Victoria he averaged 138 runs and 11 wickets for every match the two States played. Against

Dr Grace's touring side in the 1892 Test in Sydney Giffen took ten wickets in the two innings for 160 runs. Three years later, again in Sydney, he took 3–14 in the first innings and 5–26 in the second. Giffen retained his form long after he was dropped from Test cricket. As late as 1903, against Victoria, he scored 81 and 97 not out and captured 7–75 and 8–110. Thus he was still a good bowler of slow- to medium-spin with flight when Trumper got his 165 in Sydney in 1899 and several times he got Trumper's wicket in interstate games. In addition he had a good supporting bowler in Ernie ('Jonah') Jones, who had many glittering successes behind him against England with his very fast deliveries.

Years later we knew Jones in the Bodyline series. When our lads were taking Larwood in the ribs over a number of games he would sit on a seat in our dressing-room and with the well-known contempt of a former great for one of modern times tell us that Larwood wasn't really fast, that 'he wouldn't knock a dent in a pound of butter on a hot day'. But 'Jonah' was a character, and apart from his footling strictures on Larwood's pace was a popular fellow in our dressing-room. He was as thick through as a forest oak and, until Joe Darling came into the South Australian side, was the undisputed champion wrestler of the team. After the day's play Ernie would have a shower and then, naked, would offer to wrestle anybody. He was a tough customer, but Joe wrestled him into submission and 'Jonah' never afterwards threw out his challenges.

'Jonah', like Larwood, had begun life as a miner, in Broken Hill, and he was a powerful man. In the late 1920s, many years after his cricket prime, he was working as a docker at Port Adelaide. His companions bet him he couldn't carry two bags of wheat at once and take them up the plank to the top of the wheat stack. 'Jonah' thereupon tucked a 180-pound bag of wheat under each arm and walked them up the plank to the stack without difficulty. Joe Darling also contended that 'Jonah' was a better fast bowler than Larwood and that Jones could bowl for an hour at full stretch whereas Larwood bowled only in four- or five-over spells. (Jardine did this with the intention of always keeping Larwood fresh. He never over-bowled him.)

If 'Jonah' was a better fast bowler than the Larwood of 1932–3, which I doubt, I am glad I did not have to face him. But these opinions are often founded on loyalty to one's own generation. In any case, none of us ever doubted Larwood's action, while Jones's was frequently under suspicion. It surprised me that when he attended the Imperial Conference at Lord's in the 1960s Sir Donald Bradman should have had a film with him which he showed. It was of Larwood, and the film was reversed so that he was made to seem a left-handed bowler. At the moment of delivery the film was stopped, with Larwood's seeming left-arm in a very suspect position. 'Well, now, who do you think that is and what do you think of that?' asked Sir Donald, and the Englishmen were very confused when informed who it was. I cannot vouch for this story, but it came from such a good source that I believe it to be true. All I can say is that if there was the slightest suspicion of doubt in 1932–3 about Larwood we certainly would have 'thrown' that at the Englishmen. None of us ever thought there was the slightest suspicion about his delivery, and if this story is true I can only suggest it was another whim of the camera. Or do all fast bowlers throw? (It was just such a film, incidentally, that sealed Ian Meckiff's fate in Test cricket.)

But to return to Victor Trumper. Giffen got him, again LBW, for 45 in the return South Australian game in Sydney and Jones had him caught in the second innings for seven. Trumble caught and bowled him for 57 in Melbourne and he had two scores of 40-odd for Australia versus The Rest. That 165 was his sole first-class century in Club cricket, but he again glittered for Paddington and I found a description of his batting by Jack C. Davis, 'Not out' of the *Sydney Referee*, interesting and illuminating on the occasion of one of Trumper's most remarkable scores.

Jack Davis was undoubtedly the star Australian critic of the time, and was Australia's Neville Cardus, although his writing wasn't as flowery as Neville's. Davis was a short, dapper man, who used to wear pince-nez and a bowler hat. He was always well dressed in dark blue, and was indefatigable in his attendance at the nets and at matches. His reputation meant much

WHEN CRICKE[

335 IN 165

Mightiest 'five' of all

This is an artist's reconstruction of the mighty "fiver,"
hit by Victor Trumper at Redfern Oval 60 years ago, that
came back into the news this
week.

**The ball broke a window on the second floor of John
Hunter and Sons' shoe factory in Chalmers Street.**

The broken window has
been preserved as a mem-
orial to the great batsman
ever since.

Now the South Sydney
Leagues Club has bought
the factory and will demolish it for extensions.

But it decided this week
to mount the window in a
place of honour in the
club.

"The 'Sun-Herald' .dug
into the past to recall
Trumper's memorable inn-
ings at Redfern.

In 165 minutes that
afternoon of the 1902-
1903 season Trumper hit
335 runs (and in those
days a six counted only
as a five).

Trumper hit 22 fives and
39 · fours, and, with his
team-mate Dan Gee, put on

The Sydney
Sun-Herald's 1963
reconstruction of
Trumper's innings
against Redfern
in 1902.

BROKE GLASS

517 for the first wicket. to
bring crowds flocking to
the ground from all over
Sydney.

[Victor Trumper III and
Dan Gee III, played in the
the same school team for
Manly Christian Brothers'
College six years ago.]

On balcony

Commenting on the inn-
ings, another cricket immortal, famous barracker
"Yabba" (the late S. H. Gascoigne), said:

"In one over—a six-ball
over in those days—Vic and

Dan Gee got three fiv
each. It was a case of o
hit and one walk down t
wicket. The uninitiat
would have thought th
were walking a single."

[In that era if a batsm
hit a ball over the fence
a "five" he would have
walk down to the other e
to allow his partner to ta
strike.]

"I shall never forget
hit that landed on the b
factory.

"But another went rig
out of the southern en
of the park onto the ba
cony of a two-storey te
race of houses.

"Another landed right o
and nearly went into t
Australian XI Hotel (sin
demolished) bar in Elizabe

MEANT MINUTES

The Redfern hit of 1903

THE FAMOUS FIVER

BROKEN *line shows the flight of Victor Trumper's "five" that shattered a window in a shoe factory outside Redfern Oval.*

et. All traffic was held

The stroke that gave mper his 300 was also a : ball.' It went into a ying yard.

ecord score

Vic then retired, but old Ironsides induced him to rn to make 350; he got

By this time the 'keeper taken to bowling. He hed up one; Vic ran 10 s down to it, fell and tangled up with his bat. dless to say, he was out. By this time Dan Gee 150. He got 10 in the over. Then he also fell n. I think it was from gue.

By this time, if there was fan around the ground e were 10,000. They e 20 deep everywhere. fic had no chance of ng past.

M. A. Noble, the Aus-

tralian captain, did nothing but walk outside the crowd, watching to see in what suburb the ball was inclined to lodge.

"The side was all out for 618 in one afternoon, which is, I think, the record score for grade. They didn't start until 2.15 p.m. and were all out before six."

Yabba said: "There were, I think, ONLY six lost balls."

"If there had been sixes in those days goodness only knows what Victor would have scored, as he would have been retaining the strike.

"Even under-arms were bowled in a desperate attempt to get him out. This was the first time I had

seen them since Humphries, the English lob-bowler got wickets against Australia when I was a boy."

Spread field

"Nine fieldsmen were on the boundary to Vic—with the slip on the fence. The only men close in were the bowler and wicket-keeper."

The late H. L. "Herbie" Collins, a former Australian captain once said:

"So many of Trumper's strokes landed the ball on an adjacent bowling green that bowls play was suspended while the players lined the bank to watch Trumper."

Trumper's innings was also memorable for a sidelight on the recent "chucking" controversy.

When his batting partner complained that "the bowler was throwing the ball," Trumper took him aside and said: "Don't complain about it—they might take him off."

Present groundsman of Redfern Oval, Mr D. Wood, said that while Redfern Oval was smaller in Trumper's days, the shoe factory was in the same position.

"It must have been a mighty hit. I estimate that the ball landed 150 yards from where Victor Trumper hit it. If there had been no factory the shot would have undoubtedly travelled further" he said.

FOOTNOTE: Trumper was not asked to pay for the broken window. Instead he was entertained lavishly by the shoe company directors and taken on a tour of the factory.

to him, and he would no more have covered a Test match at Perth from Sydney, on television and from the radio, as so many did with the last West Indian tour of Australia, than take a space-craft to the moon – always supposing he'd been able to. He was one hundred per cent reliable, and thought of his reputation before committing thoughts to a newspaper. There was no idle, flimsy stuff from JCD. He weighed his opinions ultra-cautiously. Here he is on Trumper triumphant:

> The public, sensing a sensation, rolled up to the extent of over 3000 at Hampden Park where Vic Trumper gave one of the most extraordinary displays which he alone among the world's best batsmen seems capable of making. Victor Trumper and W. W. Chapman began the Paddington innings. They quickly – and Trumper particularly – had the bowlers bewildered and the fieldsmen running their legs off, speeding to the fence after the ball or vainly trying to intercept it. Trumper made 100 of 156. Chapman reached his 100 with the total at 275. Three times later, with his score at 251, Trumper stepped out to a short one and hit it on the rise to J. W. Fletcher, one of his team-mates, who was fielding as substitute at mid-on. The stroke left the impression on one's mind that Trumper wanted to get out to give one of his colleagues a strike. In an hour and 50 minutes the first wicket put on 330 runs, Trumper 215 with 33 fours and six fives.
>
> I don't remember ever having seen him play an innings like this one. Time after time he hit the ball skimming slowly like a rising swallow over the heads of fieldsmen at point, cover point, extra mid-off and mid-off. At times it seemed that he was merely having a casual knock at the nets. There was no bustling between the wickets for notches [the original expression for runs], no hurry, no excitement. Even the spectators seemed dazed by it all and applauded but slightly. At times Trumper seemed to be merely practising his strokes, to see how exactly he could place the ball out of reach of fieldsmen while lifting it. The fieldsmen were constantly shifting, but as they shifted the flight and direction of the ball were changed by the batsman until all the

fieldsmen were bewildered. All this time Trumper scarcely
turned a hair. An occasional burst of applause in appreciation of a spanking drive for five [still no sixes!] alone
enlivened the scene. It is a gorgeous thing that Trumper
lives in Sydney. If he lived in Melbourne, Adelaide or Brisbane, would we know anything of the mighty qualities of
his batsmanship? There never has been another batsman in
the same class as Trumper. Even old-stagers admit that their
champion, W. L. Murdoch, as a batsman was never in the
same class. W. G. Grace in his prime must have been as
wonderful as our champion of today for the consistency
with which he made enormous scores and his scores were
made against good bowling; but W.G. never had the beauty
of style which in Trumper is allied to perfect excellence.
One cannot compare them – as a few who saw W.G. in his
prime and who have seen our present hero will affirm.
Besides, conditions have changed so greatly from 35 years
ago.

This score of 215 that Davis waxed so poetical about was
made against Redfern. His scores over the years against this
club had been 133, 103, 118, 158, 335, 13 and 215, an aggregate
of 1075 runs at an average of 153.

It is interesting that Paddington provided a substitute in
that last innings of 215. Perhaps a bowler had had more than
his fill of Trumper, and had decided he could better be occupied
elsewhere. At all events, during Trumper's even greater innings
– of 335 – it was reported that Redfern bowlers turned their
backs on their skipper when he had an invitation for them.
And we move now to that score of 335 because it was that,
and the manner in which it was made, that turned Sydney
club cricket upside down. It was never the same again.

Sydney's notorious 'Yabba', possibly the best-known barracker the cricket world has known, said six balls were lost out
of the ground during that innings. 'Yabba's' name was Gascoigne, and he would be known in these days, I suppose, as a
'rabbitologist'. He sold rabbits from a horse-drawn cart in the
Sydney suburbs and he was followed down the streets by an

army of cats waiting for the time until 'Yabba' had a sale and would proceed to skin and gut the rabbit.

He knew cricket, and he had a good sense of humour and would often have his fellow barrackers holding their sides in laughter at his 'Ocker' wit. His great call was 'Time!' with which he used to announce his presence at a game, whereupon everybody was agog. If a slow batsman, like Kelleway, Collins or myself, got a single after a period of defence, 'Yabba' would yell: 'Blimey, he's bolted!' or 'Blimey, he's alive!' He convulsed the crowd one day when Tate, with his big feet, ran through three boots. As the last was brought out to him 'Yabba' called out: 'Eh, Maurice, thank goodness you're not a centipede.'

'Yabba' was one of those who saw Trumper bat at Redfern on the great '335' occasion. Trumper and Gee put on 517 for the first wicket, Vic hitting 22 fives and Gee ten. In one over they got three each, the most runs possible, for it was then a six-ball over and when a batsman hit a five the batsmen had to change ends. Gascoigne tells of how one of Vic's fives went right over John Hunter's boot factory. Another nearly went into the Australian XI hotel bar. Gascoigne says all the trams were held up. The stroke that gave Trumper his 300 was also 'lost'. On reaching 300 he retired, but was persuaded by an enthusiast, a Mr Ironsides, to return to see if he could get 350. The Redfern 'keeper – everybody else having been tried – went on to bowl and at 335 Trumper rushed yards down the wicket to him, got his feet all tangled up, fell over and was stumped by the 'keeper's substitute.

The Paddington side was all out for 618, the runs all coming in the one afternoon. Play didn't start until 2.15 p.m. and finished before six. The nine fieldsmen to Trumper were at one time all on the boundary: the square-leg umpire also was nearly there, as he believed in safety first. Even under-armers were bowled in a desperate attempt to get Trumper out. And in a later match he followed this with the 215 which Jack Davis has so well described.

'Yabba' passed on in the early 'sixties but people are still alive who saw that Trumper innings at Redfern in 1902–3.

Tom Ferrier, a vice-president of the Lane Cove cricket club in Sydney, says that as a boy of ten he chased two of the hits for five up towards Great Buckingham Street. He says the 'daddy' of all Trumper's hits was that one over the Hunter boot factory. On the following Monday morning a woman from Douglas Street came over and met the greenkeeper and handed him a cricket ball with the question, 'Is this the ball referred to in the paper as the one hit by Victor Trumper over Hunter's factory? I found it in my back garden.' She left the ball with the greenkeeper.

Another who watched Trumper in action at Redfern Oval that day was Sir William McKell, afterwards a NSW Premier, and Governor-General of Australia. He has a lively memory and in telling me of that afternoon related how the local Chinese shopkeepers rushed to put shutters over their windows when Trumper began his big hitting. The Chinese, chattering and excited, thought that a riot, reminiscent of earlier goldfield days, had broken out, such was the tumult. He also told me that a ball was found on the Monday *in* the boot factory, having smashed the window on the second floor. That smashed window, boarded up, remained as a memorial to Trumper for years, and when the South Sydney Leagues club built its new premises it took the window with them. The owners of the boot factory also entertained Trumper to lunch at the factory to commemorate his feat. Another Premier of NSW, James McGowan, was playing bowls on a nearby rink and the bombardment from Trumper's hits over the fence was so incessant that the bowls had to be abandoned. They watched the cricket instead.

7

Trumper's Technique

At this point an analysis of Trumper's technique is appropriate. We can do it in both words and pictures, and I am going to turn again to the words of M. A. Noble, for no one knew Trumper better. Noble was at school with him, captained him in the Paddington, NSW and Australian teams, and was a life-long admirer. He wrote at length of Trumper in his book, *The Game's the Thing*, and he used the same long chapter in a talk he gave on Trumper on Australian radio.

Strangely, however, he writes of Trumper's marvellous innings against England in Melbourne on a 'sticky' and of how he trounced Jack Saunders on another 'sticky', saying that he made 100 before lunch. That is not correct; Trumper did not open the innings but was 70-odd not out at lunch and got his century quickly after. It was odd that Noble should have made such a mistake. He also says that bowlers frequently appealed for LBW against Trumper only to find that the bat had connected at the last moment. Fast bowlers particularly appealed when they sent down a yorker on the leg-stump before Trumper removed his foot and a beautiful on-side shot resulted. Often, said Noble, he had seen great players at the other end stare with astonishment at the audacity of Trumper's strokes. Every stroke he made seemed to be absolutely correct and he was always in the best position to make it. Even when he changed his mind, which he often did, he was invariably in position and the stroke seemed the only one possible. 'In many ways,' said Noble,

he reminded me of a great orator. You follow the discourse, even anticipate correctly the word he is going to use – it all

seems so natural and easy – yet, if you try to do it yourself,
you fail miserably. He would pick up a bat everyone else
had scorned, go in and make a century with it, come out and
say : 'What is wrong with this bat ? It is a very good one.'

He never used a cover, or rubber grip for the bat handle.
He and Reggie Duff used to roughen the handle string with a
piece of glass and apply powdered resin. He disliked chamois
leather and rubber grips because, he said, they interfered with
the instinctive movement of the hands. He liked the weight
of the bat to be more in the centre back than was customary,
and for that reason would shave off some of the lower and
thicker portion of the hump in order to secure a more even
distribution of weight. Of his batting approach, Noble wrote :

Victor was a law unto himself. You could talk to him and
coach him. He would listen carefully, respect your advice
and opinions and, leaving you, would forget all you told him,
play as he wanted to play and thereby prove that, although
you might be right, he knew a better method. He would hit
the first ball of a Test match for four, if it suited him. Sometimes, but not often, this would lead to his early downfall.
It is necessary for most batsmen to play the game for a few
overs before unfolding their strokes. Not so with Victor.
He was off at the jump, making an amazing stroke off a
ball that would probably have clean bowled most of his
comrades. His defence was his offence. If, on a bad wicket,
a left-hander was troubling anyone, he would immediately
set about knocking him off, and generally succeed in doing
so.

Dr H. M. Moran comments on how quickly Trumper would
bustle from the gloom of the pavilion to the brightness of the
pitch, which, in the opinion of all batsmen, is wrong, because
the eyes have not become accustomed to the sunlight or the
pace and height of the pitch, and, being unaware of the
characteristics of the bowler, Trumper might attempt a back-
cut, easy enough later on but difficult at the moment. The ball,

perhaps doing something unexpected, would be edged into the slips or behind the wickets. Again, in a fast-bowler's over, he might make a pull shot off a straight ball just short of a good length, a ball which, making pace and lifting quickly and high off the pitch, would be mistimed and edged, giving a catch close in on the on-side.

One of his maxims used to be: 'Spoil a bowler's length and you've got him.' And a very sound maxim it is, for no kind of bowling is any use unless it is of good length. Invariably he put his precept into practice. Sometimes, however, he did meet a bowler who kept his length despite Victor's onslaught. This did not stop him, though it made it harder for him to make his wonder strokes and perhaps slowed down his rate of scoring.

Noble thought the most marvellous quality about Trumper was that he was able to reveal his genius when he was 'up against it'. When batsmen of international or other calibre were in sore distress on a bad, fiery or crumbling wicket, he always appeared to be most at ease. His best efforts were frequently made on such wickets, and against bowlers able to extract the last ounce of assistance from them.

The reason for this, Noble thought, was to be found in his attention to and concentration on the bowler's fingers just before delivery of the ball. He could invariably spot the over-spin from a left-hander, and instead of shaping for a leg-break was ready for the straight one that skidded through. He would then at once walk in front of the wicket and strike it to the on-side where the fieldsmen were few. Dealing with a good length ball just outside the off stump, breaking away, he would sometimes let it go, but not often; and the way he would follow the course of the break and late-cut it for four was a sight for the batsman at the other end to marvel at. The most difficult and dangerous strokes were made with consummate ease, yet his action was so free that onlookers were often deceived into the belief that he was facing the easiest of bowlers. You really had to be batting with him to realize his ability to the full.

On a bad wicket, Trumper would never allow bowlers to make him play at the blind spot, to be beaten by break off

"Auckland"
Help St
Chatwood
3/2/13

Dear Master Coningsby
I am pleased
to receive your letter & have to thank
you for your kind wishes. "With
Ball & Bat" by Geo Giffen is very interesting
& contains valuable advice on the game
In his best days Geo Giffen was the
best all round Australian player & his
performances are splendid not only
from a cricket point of view but as
a very strong athlete. Giffen's fore &
upper right arm is bigger than Jack
Lyons who is both taller & considerably
heavier than Giffen. To advance in
the game you must lead a good
healthy life. Dr. W.G. Grace is still
a non smoker. Avoid alcohol for
it will tell on a players constitution
sooner or later When practising
watch the ball very carefully in
fact never take your eyes off it.

---

mper's letter of 3 February 1913 to an aspiring schoolboy cricketer.

G

When playing in a
match Keep in your minds eye
the exact position if every fielder.
To learn fielding
join a baseball club.
Do not copy any
player but when you see him
score four off a ball try & score
a four off that ball in the
same direction but do it
your own way for that
will be the natural way for you

Be very particular not
to let Sport interfere with your
work for Sport only lasts for awhile
whereas your work must Keep you
in comfort or otherwise just as you
treat it. I think I have given
you the ABC. Dont let Sport
worry you. If it does give it up.
With all good wishes
Remain
Yours
Victor Trumper

the pitch. He would go down the pitch, turning the ball into a harmless half-volley. He played left-handers on a bad wicket in a measure similar to his treatment of slow leg-break bowlers on good wickets. When facing a ball just short of a good length on the off stump, breaking away to the slips, Trumper would step right across to the off-side and, meeting it as it broke, would pull it away from the numerous fieldsmen on the off, right across the wicket to the on-side. The bowler, believing his length to be short, quite naturally pitched the next time a little farther up. Instantly, Trumper would jump into it and make a suitable forcing stroke.

Victor always acted on the principle that it was a fatal error to 'scratch' forward at a slow bowler (he would rarely come across one of them today). His anticipation of the pitch of the ball was uncanny, and his decision to use a particular stroke was made so early in the ball's flight that, being also quick footed, he was yards down the pitch before another less-gifted batsman would have decided upon the stroke to be made. That was the reason for his success in making full tosses and half-volleys of balls which might easily have been fatal had they been allowed to hit the pitch. This method of attack had the effect of making the bowler drop them shorter, and then, by stepping back and getting into proper position, he could hit them just where he pleased. This is how he knocked them off their length.

Sometimes, when he had jumped out, the ball would drop shorter than anticipated and, being unable to make a full-toss or half-volley of it, he would change the direction of his stroke. He would follow the course of its break, and make a long, low hit over the covers and between the out-fields, if necessary lifting it right over the off-side fence; but, said Noble, he used this stroke only when he found it impossible to place the ball correctly. If this was deemed too risky he frequently changed his mind, and while the ball was in flight could come right back and use the cut to great purpose.

His method of dealing with 'bosie' bowling was simple, and Noble illustrates the method of all notable batsmen, I think, in how they played this off-break delivered with a leg-break action. Trumper did not bother about trying to detect the spin action. If he could get out to it the 'bosie' did not matter, and if it were bowled short there was plenty of time to detect and deal with it after it left the pitch.

Noble says Trumper's ability to score quickly off medium-paced bowling was amazing. Instead of playing forward in the orthodox way Trumper would surprise the bowler by getting across the wicket and, with a straight bat, hit a good-length ball on the rise from the pitch outside the off stump with great force and along the ground between mid-on and square-leg. This stroke was made possible because of his perfect timing and his exceptionally strong wrists. If mid-on were moved to a wider and more forward position to block this stroke Trumper would at once make a far easier stroke, between the bowler and mid-on. If mid-on were brought back and square-leg brought forward to fill the gap he would wait for the good-length ball pitched on the wicket, not outside the off stump, and would hit it past the square-leg umpire like a flash. In this manner, he was always beating the fieldsmen.

Noble says the marvel of Trumper's placing was such that he did not remember his ever being caught close in on the on-side, though hundreds of times the ball was in the air when passing the fieldsmen. Seeing ball after ball hit in this way, the bowler was apt to conclude that he was pitching them on the short side and so would pitch them up a little more. Then Trumper would sprint down the pitch and drive them any-where he pleased. His remarkable on-side play obviated the necessity of using the cut, which always possessed an element of danger. Trumper could cut, but most of the fieldsmen were on the off. Noble knew of no stroke in cricket of which Trumper was not absolute master. That, he admits, is a big claim to make for any batsman, but he made it unreservedly because (writing in 1926, which was pre-Bradman) he had seen nearly all the great batsmen of the last forty years, from Grace downwards, and had seen none to equal Trumper.

Noble writes of the difficulties of playing leg-theory, which is so cramping to the batsmen, and the danger of using certain strokes, and describes how Trumper would run down the pitch, draw away and force or cut it to the off-side where, probably, only one fieldsman would be stationed. The wrist power behind these cuts, made from an awkward position and against a ball travelling at pace, was astonishing.

Noble's description of how Trumper set out after a slow bowler also exactly fits Bradman. The two champions had much in common. Bradman had an unusual top or left-hand grip of the bat. His fingers faced the bowler more than those of any batsman I knew but it gave him a tremendous advantage, enabling him to turn the bat face over immediately after pulling the ball. It was because of this that he was so strong on the on-side and rarely, if ever, did he get caught on the pull.

Bradman, too, could play any stroke. There was obviously no comparison between the two in grace and beauty of stroke but the Don was a hard-headed customer who judged himself and everybody else by runs. He didn't care a fig for so-called grace or beauty. He was a realist. But why was Trumper so head and shoulders over Bradman on a 'sticky' wicket, as he so obviously was? It seems odd that in this one area he was more of a realist than Bradman because Bradman was very long-headed in most things. The answer is that Trumper went about learning how a 'sticky' wicket would play. He had many friends on the staff of the Sydney Cricket Ground and none more staunch than J. Jennings, who was ground curator from 1899 to 1911. Vic asked Jennings, who readily co-operated, whether he could prepare a special 'sticky' wicket at the Sydney nets. Jennings could, and did. On the edge of the strip of Sydney practice pitches Jennings used the hose freely, and before Victor went in on the good pitch he went in on the 'sticky' which, under the influence of a hot sun, kicked and bucked. That was one reason Trumper was so proficient on them. He knew what to expect.

Don Bradman, usually so thorough, did not go to such trouble. His whole background had been on hard pitches and he reasoned that 'stickies' were few and far between and he would take his luck with them, especially as covered pitches were beginning to come into favour. He had no liking for a bad pitch – indeed, to the contrary : I remember him in Brisbane being caught on one one day after a big score the day before. He showed obvious concern and his innings finished when he knocked over his stumps from behind them.

Bradman also reasoned that a good pitch would be along in quick time and then he would obliterate a temporary failure. The covered wickets banished 'stickies' for the most part, which was a great pity in many ways, though of course I realize the need to cover pitches to ensure play and 'the gate'.

A 'sticky' was more than a test of a batsman's skill and courage, however. It was a supreme test of a captain's knowledge of how much rain had fallen, its dependence upon the future of the weather, what effect sunshine would have upon it, and many other factors, including declarations. Covered pitches have made it much easier for captains.

Whereas most batsmen I knew who could handle 'stickies' used to change their technique, it was interesting that Trumper didn't. Others would move their grip lower down the handle, concentrating on defence and the pull shot, but Trumper never changed from his high grip of the bat. Elliott Monfries, who kept wicket for Victoria against Trumper, said most of his forward run-getting strokes were made with a rhythmic golf-like swing that started and finished high over his head. 'When first he batted in front of me,' said Monfries, 'I remember thinking, If you do that again and the ball does anything, you'll get yourself out. But when the ball did do anything it seemed to make no difference whatever as it found itself plumb in the centre of the bat and sailing out into the field.' Monfries never found out why, on a 'sticky', Trumper could still use the long round-the-body swing and use it with the utmost success. 'With such a batsman as Clem Hill, who gripped his bat low and used a short swing, one felt that one would never get him out.' Trumper's style of batting, however, often convinced wicket-keepers that he would get *himself* out.

In 1964 I saw an old movie of Trumper batting. It was interesting in that it showed the great man at the wicket, but I got the impression that he was improvising strokes and not taking the occasion seriously. That was far from the case in the series of strokes he performed for Fry and Beldam for their book on batting (*Great Batsmen: Their Methods at a Glance*, 1905), a fascinating study of batsmen of Trumper's period and their strokes. That astute man Richie Benaud first of all drew my attention to the master picture of all, Trumper jumping down the pitch to drive. It is a much-used photograph, but Benaud suggested to me that the picture was a fake because it pretended to be of Trumper in a match and it was nothing of the sort. There is no other person in the picture, no fieldsman, no square-leg umpire, no one.

I accept Benaud's opinion that it is a fake, though it greatly disappointed me because I had once written that the picture is so inspiring it should be hung in all the cricket dressing-rooms of the world; but no matter. The photograph is still so perfect in the smallest detail, the back-swing, the arms, the balance of the body, the movement forward of the weight and general poise, that any talk of faking by the photographer is immaterial.

The beauty of the Trumper photographs, so many taken on the Nursery practice ground at Lord's, is that they so clearly reveal his technique, his correctness, and his range of strokes. I notice in the collection there is not one of the dog-shot so perhaps we can accept that Trumper did not think very much of the stroke which got him out so often and had no wish to include it.

The first picture is of Trumper's stance at the crease (I will not reproduce this, as the front cover of the present book illustrates the same point). Plum Warner was the only critic of the photo I could find. He said that Trumper's bend of the right knee was ugly; but I can't agree. A batsman can't stand at the crease with a stiff left or right leg. Trumper had a bend in his right leg to give him spring, balance, and correct distribution of weight. He is at the ready in his stance to play either back or forward. His hold of the bat is higher on the handle than that of most batsmen, but the hands – importantly – are together, working as one and not pulling against each other. The right hand is ready to move down to the bottom of the handle for a hook, a pull, or a defensive stroke. The full left eye and most of the right look at the bowler, but although the head is turned almost full face to the bowler he is careful not to allow his shoulders to turn to a two-eyed position, which is the cardinal error of many batsmen and leads to them playing across the line of flight of the ball. His back foot points to point; his front foot to cover. The cutting line of his toes points a straight line down the pitch so that they are in the accepted correct position, neither in advance nor retreat of each other.

In the seventh photograph, which I have reproduced, we have Trumper playing a pull. Again he has taken himself, by footwork, into the perfect position. The ball is short and outside the off stump. The pull is aimed square. This stroke foxed me when I played it and got me into much trouble. Looking back, I can see that the fault lay in not getting into the correct position, in not going across the pitch and back with my back foot so that I could get outside the line of the ball and unlock my shoulders.

I watched Wally Hammond when young and greatly admired the way in which he hit a short ball on the off through the covers. It was Wally's favourite stroke and those who remember him will recall that he never shone, as I saw him, on the pull shot. To play this cover forcing stroke Hammond moved his back foot back towards the stumps and certainly not across the wicket. His body had to be clear so that his bat could swing up and down in a vertical fashion. This locks the shoulders and doesn't unpin them as Trumper does in his pull shot. I travelled with Dennis Lillee from Perth to Melbourne on Christmas Day 1975, and he was very eager to know all about the fast bowlers I had played against. I happened to mention to him that I was weak on the pull, and explained that my weakness was obviously brought about by getting into Hammond's habit of stepping back towards the stumps. Dennis drooled, and I can imagine how he would have loved to have bowled at me. It is imperative, as Trumper demonstrates, to move across the pitch to open the shoulders. His alteration of the grip on the bat with the bottom hands gives him full control of the bat, as this is very much a bottom-handed shot. His weight is perfect. He swings his left foot high but for all the part the left leg plays in the shot, after pushing it right across and transferring his weight, he could well have put it in his pocket.

I note that Charles Fry describes photos seven and eight in this series as hooks. We held many discussions, mostly in fun, in our dressing-room about hooks and pulls, and we could rarely agree on the difference. Trumper was obviously both a great hooker and puller, and these plates bear careful study by the enthusiast. I only wish I could reproduce them all.

The ninth picture is a perfect illustration of the beginning of an off-drive. Trumper's weight is obviously coming into the stroke at the right moment and I like the perfect movement of his shoulders pointing in the same direction as his left toe and pointing towards the direction the ball will take. As in all his strokes there is no lifting or tilting of the head: like a good golfer, his head is always perfectly still and kept on the same plane.

Number eleven is full of vitality, with one jump at the ball, as Fry says, for a straight drive. Fry likes the way Trumper keeps his arms near his body, and it is to be noted again that Trumper's swing is co-ordinated and under control, with no suggestion of overswing. His front foot comes down correctly to the ball and the weight is on his front foot – as is well demonstrated in the next picture, which shows the completion of the previous drive.

Number fifteen illustrates one of Trumper's dangerous yet exhilarating strokes, the pull drive. The ball is outside the off stump and is lifted right round between mid-on and square-leg. The right shoulder and knee are dropped as there is no attempt to keep the ball down.

I never saw in my time a better cutter of the ball than my Waverley and NSW captain, Alan Kippax. As a youth, I travelled one night in a tram with him from Bondi Junction, and, awed at being in the great man's presence, asked him about his renowned late-cut. I don't know whether Alan thought that I expected him to get up in the rocking, rolling tram around Centennial Park and demonstrate his late-cut, but he told me to forget all about it; he said it was too risky and

had got him out too often. Yet Kippax played it like the true
artist he was. He was one of the best stroke-players I have seen.
I have seen none to compare with him in the late-cut as he
would allow the ball to get almost past him and then bring his
bat down from between his head and his shoulders and give
the ball a delicious late flick and it would go down and away
with amazing speed.

I would think that Kippax, who saw a lot of Trumper, would
have emulated him in this stroke. In number twenty-two
Trumper has just completed a late cut and the bat has come
down as I have described Kippax's stroke. Fry says the ball
is played much more on the stumps than most batsmen would
like, but points out that Trumper has given himself plenty of
room for the shot and has been able to place his feet well.
The shot is made mostly by the wrists with the body well over
the ball.

Fry gives other illustrations of Trumper's varied strokes but
these appeal to me as the principal ones and demonstrate
excellently Trumper's main strokes and how he achieved them.
The conception of the stroke was in Trumper's agile and alert
mind and shows why he was such an attraction to watch. His
art did not come easily to him; he had to work hard to
achieve the fundamentals of batting; but, once learned, he went
on to show to what heights the art could rise.

How would Victor Trumper have fared against Bodyline? It is
an interesting thought and, understandably, the old-timers
about when we had the job of facing up to it used to throw
up their hands to the cricket heavens and declare he would
have decimated it.

I have strong doubts. We made a bigger mess of the job
than we should have done, and a few who gorged themselves
in a gargantuan manner when the pitches were true and the
bowling orthodox should have been more prepared than they
were to battle against Bodyline. But I withdraw nothing of
what I wrote in my first book, *Cricket Crisis*, in which I
declared with all the vehemence of youth that not even
Trumper could have handled it. However, I would like to add

to what I wrote then.

Larwood and Voce, now two good friends of mine, were made to suffer too much. Had we pelted it back Bodyline would have died in one match, for all Douglas Jardine's stubbornness. His batsmen would have driven him to drop it, though Warner, one of the two England managers, afterwards complained that he could do nothing with Jardine (who in later years I found to be a warm man with a rare sense of ironic humour).

The fossilized doctors and aged legal men who were in charge of Australian cricket in those days made a mess of the footling cables they sent to England. Billy Woodfull told me himself years afterwards that perhaps he was wrong in the attitude he took, that he should have listened to Vic Richardson, his vice-captain, who wanted to bounce them back at the English. One day Wally Hammond got out to a short ball at Adelaide, and as he walked back with thunderous brow to the pavilion he said: 'If this is what the bloody game is coming to it's time a man got out of it.' So there is reason to believe that the English would have done no better against the bouncers than us. But writing as a chap of meagre ability who had struggled to a few top scores against England up to Adelaide (Jardine recognized a weakness I had outside the off stump, switched to that angle and had me out for none each innings before I woke up to the fact that he had forsaken Bodyline against me), I was not very impressed with one or two of the others who were not prepared to battle it through, and said so in that first book.

Don Bradman, who of course was Target Number One of Bodyline, took exception to my criticisms and, on looking back, I cannot blame him for his first consideration – getting himself and his head out of the way. I consider that the sickening blow over the heart that Larwood gave Billy Woodfull at Adelaide could have led to Woodfull dropping dead when he did, in the spring of 1965, coming up the 18th hole of a Brisbane golf course. Woodfull, who neither smoked nor drank, should by rights have lived to a ripe old age.

One story, I think, I owe to myself. The day Woodfull was

hit that awful blow, Warner and Palairet, the other English manager, came into our room to commiserate with him. It was then that Woodfull made his famous statement about two teams being out on the field, one playing cricket and the other not, and, routed, the two English managers fled our room. Harold Larwood told me later that Warner blamed me for leaking that story to the Press and promised Larwood a pound if he got me out for nil in the second innings, which Larwood did.

Subsequently Warner, who sat on the fence 'with his ears close to the ground', as one of our politicians once put it, blamed me publicly for the leak. Writing of the story, Warner said: 'Unfortunately, a member of the Australian team was also a Pressman, and next day the story was blazoned all over the front pages.' That was certainly pointing the bone at me, and the thought that I had leaked from the dressing-room did me no good at all. Well, the story as told me by Claude Corbett, then writing for the *Sun* and a colleague of mine, was this: 'I got a ring on the phone that night at our hotel. It was from Don Bradman, who told me he wanted to tell me something. Don was also working in a third-sense for the *Sun*, being associated with a broadcasting firm and a sports store. We arranged a rendezvous on North Terrace and, while we sat in his car, he told me all about the Warner–Woodfull incident. It was too hot a story to run on my own, and I gave it to all the Press.'

I have always held it against the Don that he did not own up and clear me. Warner himself had a cheek to think such a sensational story would not leak out, as there were several in the team who maintained a 'leaking' connection with the Press.

Bradman obviously didn't like what I wrote about him in *Cricket Crisis* and for years ignored me. Then one night we were both with the English team at dinner at Government House, Perth, and throughout the evening we studiously ignored each other. I thought it all too silly and wrote the Don accordingly, and we agreed to bury the hatchet. No doubt this explanation will unearth the old feud again, but I think I owe it to myself to tell the story as Claude Corbett told it me. At least Don Bradman was a very good and observant reporter. He had every detail correct.

This, of course, is by way of digression, though it may serve to remind one yet again of the strong feelings that were aroused by the Bodyline business. So, if Bradman could not tackle Bodyline, could Victor Trumper?

When I was seeking information for the present book, I had a letter from Gordon Mallett, of Beacon Hill, NSW, and he sent me an article written by J. W. Fletcher who played with, and was secretary of, the Paddington club in its great days. He wrote along the lines of players picking up the art of batsmanship from established players they had seen. Charlie Macartney, one of our greatest, copied the art of Trumper. Kippax learnt his art, also, from Trumper; Archie Jackson copied Kippax and so the line went on – Greg Chappell being in the same Trumper mould.

'There was little or no coaching in those days,' ran Fletcher's article. 'Excessive coaching deadens the game. It should be confined to young schoolboys and then only those boys who possess natural ability and keenness. They should be able to acquire for themselves the art of batsmanship, with only an odd fault corrected here and there. But the early rudiments of the game need to be taught by a sound coach.'

He quotes Fry and Cardus as the great writers of the game and agrees with them in singling out Grace, Ranjitsinhji, Trumper and Bradman as the greatest batsmen the game has known (why no Hobbs?). Fletcher says that these four all varied their play, in different ages of the game, on changing pitches and against bowlers of varying calibre and technique. He warily approaches the question he sets himself : which was the greatest?

He plumps for Trumper because of his marvellous ability on bad and sticky pitches. 'It often depended on the state of the game whether Victor would produce his great ability. He knew that no one was his equal on bad wickets whereas, on good ones, he often left it to others, or gave his wicket away if others were doing well, and the game was safe. He always played for his side, never for himself, and averages did not concern him.'

Fletcher goes on to observe, and I agree with him in this: 'It is a pity that wickets are now covered, as the bad wickets, when they happened, showed up the great players and the game was more sporting.'

Then he goes into rhapsodies about Trumper. 'He was a master of all the strokes. His timing and placing of the ball could not have been excelled. On almost all occasions, he went in first and was aggressive from the outset. Thus he gave the bowlers a chance. I could not imagine him blocking the ball for a maiden over, which is so often seen today.'

Fletcher said he had often been asked how Trumper would have fared against Larwood and his Bodyline. Fletcher saw Stan McCabe's immortal 187 not out against the English in Sydney against the bouncers and the close leg ring of fieldsmen. McCabe, he said, never flinched. He goes on:

> He had the power, the courage and aggressiveness, he came to light when difficulties arose. McCabe and Trumper had many things in common. Victor would have followed the same course as McCabe pursued. He would have broken up the field to suit his choice. He would have broken up the short-leg field for certain. He had the power, the courage, and so great a gift for placing the ball that he would have demoralized the field, thus making the leg-side placing innocuous. He would have defied the English. He would have accepted the challenge.

With all due respect to the memory of Mr Fletcher, he is talking balderdash. Stan McCabe pierced the leg-side field on one occasion, and he would have been the first to admit that everything went his way that Saturday in Sydney, but Stan never afterwards knew a similar success. The leg-side field was too much for him, and I have no doubt that it would have been too much for Trumper too. We must also note that Strudwick stressed that Trumper had one weakness – he was

supposed not to have liked the fast ball coming into him – and
he would have got plenty of those from Bill Voce, who, in his
way, was as lethal as Larwood.

But, supposing I had to choose the Australian team from
all-time to combat Bodyline – and still believing that, had our
fast bowlers copied the English tactics, Bodyline would not
have lasted more than one Test – I would choose this side:
Victor Trumper, Keith Stackpole (who once, in a series of
pulls, took a brilliant 15 in an Adelaide Test in the opening
over off John Snow but who would have to hurry up his hook
and pull against Larwood), Stan McCabe, Charlie Macartney,
Joe Darling (whose innings of 160, when he forced the fast
bowler, Tom Richardson, to have three men in the outfield
must have been one of the greatest innings of all time), Ian
Chappell (skipper), Len Darling, Hanson Carter, Lillee, Lindwall, Thomson and Bill O'Reilly (but not for his batting).

Ian Chappell might be surprised at being chosen skipper,
but Jardine would have wondered what was going on as Ian
would set out with a purpose to 'sledge', the modern term for
on-field chat and back-chat. Carter I have included for his
famous over-the-shoulder shovel shot – and he would have
welcomed the chance to swap punches with Larwood. As a
boy of 12 I sat on the Hill at Waverley one day and saw
Carter slaughter Jack Scott, a fast round-arm bowler of fiery
temperament who later became a Test umpire, was once stood
down in Sydney club cricket for misbehaviour, and later
formed the 'establishment' in Adelaide with Bradman and Bill
Jeanes, the secretary of the Board. My friend Len Darling
might not make the final side (Verity used to worry him), but
he was a great puller and a man of tempered steel. We were
touring mates in South Africa and teamed up again in the
Melbourne Centenary Test, where he was the essence of
kindness.

I haven't included Don Bradman in my Bodyline side, but
that will not displease him. He didn't like the theory – none
of us did – but he took no pains to hide his thoughts and
reactions to it. But, thinking of what Strudwick said of
Trumper and the way he pulled away from Foster, I doubt

whether he would have done any better for all that was claimed of him and what Mr Fletcher thought of how he would have broken up the leg-side field. If one of the six men in short positions on the leg didn't get you you could be sure one of the two long fine-legs would.

8

Two Fine Innings

One of the greatest Test matches ever played between England and Australia was that at Sydney from 11 to 17 December 1903, which England deservedly won by five wickets. Fry, MacLaren and Jackson were not available for this team, the first the MCC sent to Australia, and Ranjitsinhji had played his last Test against Australia at Old Trafford in 1902. He had not been forgiven for that attack of nerves at a vital stage.

This match was to be remarkable for brilliant centuries by R. E. Foster and Trumper, sound, sensible centuries by Braund and M. A. Noble, and probably the worst crowd scenes that have ever been witnessed on any Australian ground. At one stage Plum Warner was almost on the verge of walking his English team off the field. But of that more in a moment.

Australia began batting in this 1903 Test but were soon in trouble, Duff, Trumper and Hill, the batting darlings of the Australians, all being out for twelve. M. A. Noble was by now the Australian captain, having taken over from Joe Darling, and he played a magnificent skipper's knock of 133, the Australians making 285. All the same, his captaincy in this game was to have its shortcomings, as we shall see.

Now Sydney, to my mind, is the best batting pitch and has the best light of any ground in the world. On some English grounds it is very difficult to sight the ball against the crowd and the background. At Kennington Oval, for example, I have seen more catches dropped than on any other Test ground, but Sydney is superb in the pace and trueness of its pitch and its fast, true outfield. Once a batsman gets the 'feel' of the Sydney pitch he is in his element, and life has never seemed so good with the flags of all the cricketing nations flying on top of the

H

grandstands, the sun shining brilliantly, and the dense masses on the Hill and stands providing a brilliant kaleidoscope.

Against this splendid background R. E. Foster, in his first Test innings, was to beat the Australian score on his own. Neville Cardus wrote that he was regarded without question as one of the three or four really great batsmen of the early 1900s and described him as the only batsman who used a bat quicker than Ranjitsinhji. As a freshman, he played four times at Lord's, making a brilliant 171 in 1900, the record individual score in the University match up till that time. Ten days later, for the Gentlemen versus the Players, again at Lord's, he scored 102 not out and 136 in the same match. Business kept him out of cricket for many years and he had to refuse to lead the Englishmen in Australia in 1907–8. He never played against Australia in England. His innings of 287 in Sydney was the then record individual Test score. It occupied him just under seven hours and had 38 boundaries in it. Neville Cardus wrote, 'Cricketers who saw his cutting at Sydney that day agreed it was incomparable for rapidity, touch and effortlessness.'

At the end of the second day England were 243 for four, Foster not out 73, Braund not out 67. Foster at this stage had batted almost three hours. He was uncertain at first and was missed off Saunders at mid-off when 51.

There were thunderstorms during the night but the wicket was true and fast next day, almost as fast as Foster. He got to his century just before Braund reached his, but with England 332 for eight soon after lunch Australia were still well in the game.

Partnered by Relf, Foster hopped into the Australian attack and made 94 between lunch and tea, remarkably fast scoring, and if Noble was the great captain most claimed he was one wonders why he didn't restrict the English rate of scoring by more conservative field placing, an inner and outer ring. But even worse was in store for the Australian bowlers – and for Noble's captaincy. Relf left at 447 and then Foster and Rhodes, last man in, so dominated the Australian attack that they put on a record 130 for the last wicket in only 66 minutes. Well as Foster must have batted one cannot understand how Noble and his men allowed the Englishmen to run such riot. Rhodes, of course, was not the typical No. 11 batsman. Later he was to open with great credit for England.

J. C. Davis, in the *Referee*, found himself disappointed in Foster's first hundred:

A very valuable and solid innings. It was not, however, the class of cricket expected from a batsman of Foster's reputation for brilliancy, more especially after he had become well set. His best strokes were on the off-drive. Braund displayed more versatility than Foster and though he, too, was deadly serious in his play, his was the finer cricket, fewer faulty strokes and better timing marking his play generally.

But Davis found much to commend on the Monday, the third day:

Foster and Braund, after a few quiet overs, commenced to force runs more than they did on Saturday. Braund was the more aggressive, but Foster got runs with almost equal quickness, his clever placing making up for Braund's success in high-driving. Foster and Braund added 192 runs for the fifth wicket. Braund did not give a chance, made lots of beautiful strokes on the drive and cut and used the high drive with judgement and skill. At the time of Braund's dismissal Foster had also made 102, but had been at the wickets an hour and four minutes longer. It is the best batting Braund has ever showed on the Sydney ground.

At luncheon, the game had turned quickly as, at this point, England, with three wickets still to fall, led by only 33 runs and, despite the fine play of Foster and Braund, only 75 runs had been added between noon and 1.30 p.m., Foster making 36 in an hour and 25 minutes. He had now been at the wickets 4 hours and 25 minutes for his 109.

Once again, as at Manchester a little time before, Hill caught Lilley on a grand catch. Hill couldn't sight the ball, ran the wrong way, was re-directed by his fellows and brought off a good catch. 'With eight wickets down for 332 things were not so bad after all from the Australian point of view: but this English team is never out until the tenth wicket goes down – the last two wickets added 245.' Davis disappoints me in this. He might have given rein to his imagination and knowledge and left behind, on the shores of cricket time, some footprints to explain all those runs, Foster's batting, and the Australian bowling and tactics, or lack of them. It is obvious Noble and his men cracked under the strain.

Even though Rhodes even then was a good batsman, Foster, in full flow, should have at least been starved of the strike.

Relf, evidently playing to instructions, merely defended his wicket for some considerable time, and was there 20 minutes before making his first run. This not only worried the bowlers, but kept his end up while Foster, now thoroughly master of the situation, let himself go with a freedom that had not marked his earlier batting.

Relf had gone in at 2.34 and when he was neatly caught in the slips by Armstrong off Saunders in the last over before 4 o'clock adjournment, the score had been increased to 447 – 115 having been added in an hour and 24 minutes. Relf, at first stonewalling, later displayed capital form, driving ably and cutting very finely. His 31 was a distinctly heady and most valuable piece of batting, and not to be judged by the fact of the runs having taken 84 minutes to compile.

Foster now went bald-headed for everything. He passed Ranji's previous highest score against Australia of 175 and was applauded warmly from all parts of the ground. Next was Syd Gregory's 201 – appropriately, Syd was bowling at the time – and again the warmest of applause. W. L. Murdoch's 211 at the Oval was next to be passed, and on and on Foster surged, Rhodes being utterly dependable. Foster hit at everything, knowing that his luck was in as well as his eye.

Noble and his bowlers could not slow the pace nor shut the game down and eventually Foster, at 287, skied one off Howell and Noble took the catch. 'The highest score in a Test match

and, of course, the highest by an Englishman in Australia,'
wrote Davis. 'He hit 37 fours and was at the wicket 7 hours
and 10 minutes. On Saturday he batted just under three hours
for 71; on Monday about 4½ hours for 216 . . . Friday's form
didn't suggest a big innings; (but) there was no doubt about
the greatness of Foster's play on Monday. While the off-
driving and forcing strokes to the on were of a very high
order, the quality of his batting which more than any other
struck one was the placing of the ball to beat the field on both
sides of the wicket, and behind it as well. In the matter of
brilliancy and versatility of stroke, the innings would be hard
to beat.' But Davis does not comment on Noble's captaincy.
Although the responsibility thrust upon him as a batsman
because of the failure of the Australian early batsmen undoubtedly affected Noble's bowling, Davis says he was the
best of eight tried. But Trumper bowled seven overs for only
12 runs.

Now came the fourth day of the Test, the Tuesday, a day
made unforgettable by Trumper's artistry in what his team-
mates claimed was the greatest innings ever played on a good
wicket: and a day made memorable by the Hill run out and
the deplorable exhibition of bad sportsmanship by the crowd
towards the Victorian umpire, Bob Crockett.

Davis says the weather was the best of the match. Again a big
crowd was present, the gate proceeds up to then being £3500,
'of which no less a sum of about £1000 goes to the trustees of
the ground, who, it may be added, do not defray any of the
expenses.' Davis might have added that they, however, have
to get the ground and the pitch ready and clean the ground up
after each day's play. Trumper did not open, Gregory and
Kelly doing that on a pitch which had begun to turn dusty but
which had been bound again by frequent showers during the
several nights. Kelly played Arnold on and Duff went in and
he and Gregory gave an admirable display of batsmanship
before lunch. They negotiated Hirst, Arnold and Bosanquet,
but Braund and Rhodes came on just before lunch and with
success: Gregory, who had batted neatly, was caught at the
wicket. Duff had made 42 at lunch, and afterwards he and Hill

added 72 at a run a minute. The cricket, be it noted, was exhilarating enough to whip up the enthusiasm of the on-lookers who could see Australia turning this into a rare fight. Rhodes had gone off and the English attack, accordingly, lacked accuracy. With the score 184, Hill had made 34 and Duff 80 but at 191, with Duff 84, he holed out to Relf, fielding up close to Rhodes. Enter Trumper at twenty minutes to four. Rhodes, in a stirring piece of bowling, had taken 2–9 off seven overs. Australia were still 101 runs in arrears and on an obviously dusty pitch Rhodes and Hirst were keeping the Australians very quiet. At tea the batting pride of Australia, Trumper and Hill, were still there. Hopes began to rise. Hill was 46, Trumper seven. It was perhaps the slowest start Trumper ever made to a big innings. He took well into twenty minutes to get to double figures but no one worried about that. While Trumper was there Australia were still in business.

Davis says that Trumper and Hill played some choice cricket after tea, though Hill's share was principally defensive play and great speed between the wickets, a point to be noted because this quick but somewhat risky running between the wickets had whipped the spectators into a frenzy of excitement. Trumper got runs off Relf but Rhodes kept him quiet. Braund came on for Relf and his first over was the most sensational of the match and, no doubt, of the whole season. Trumper cleverly placed the first two balls through the slips to the fence, the slips being deserted. How the crowd roared in exhilaration! The next ball, Braund tried a fast one but it was a full toss on the leg, got past both Trumper and 'keeper Lilley and sped to the fence – another four. Again the crowd roared and clapped in sheer ecstasy. Warner took his time, trying to compose his fieldsmen and Braund, and put a man into the slips. The fourth ball Trumper played past extra cover for another four, the fifth back quietly to the bowler. Trumper played the last ball of the over past mid-off and the batsmen had run three when Hirst returned the ball to Braund. Braund threw the ball at the wicket while they were running the fourth, which would have made twenty off the over; Braund missed the stumps with his throw and the batsmen set out for the fifth run, being urged on by the demented crowd, and ignoring the rather sound running principle : 'Never run for a fumble.'

Well, Trumper and Hill, who had been taking all manner of such running risks, thought they were right, even though in running the fourth run Hill had over-shot his crease by yards and had much 'dead' ground to make good. Relf had backed up, stopped Braund's throw, and threw to Lilley from the scoreboard side of the ground. Lilley put the stumps down and umpire Crockett put his hand up. Hill was out in sensational circumstances at a pulsating moment in cricket history. Pandemonium broke out.

Hill, at full speed, had over-run his mark by many yards and when he turned to see that he had been given out he seemed dumbfounded. The onlookers obviously took their cue from the batsman. Davis, who shared the general opinion that Hill had made good his ground, said the spectators for a few minutes could not realize that he was out. Davis then continues his story :

But after Hill had walked about 20 yards, booing against the umpire was started in the Pavilion. It continued for some time, and the English captain left the wicket and came in towards the pavilion, and apparently appealed to the noisy ones. While one must say that the decision against Hill appeared to be incorrect, Hill seemingly almost being level with the wicket when it was put down, the demonstration against the umpire was most unsportsmanlike, and coming from the Members' Pavilion (though only a section of it) made one blush. Though Hill walked off in a manly way when he found the decision was against him there could be no misconstruing his dejected appearance – it was plain he thought that the umpire had made a mistake. But the umpire is there to make such a decision; he was in a better position than anybody else to see what had happened, and though one will always feel that he erred it is to be deeply regretted that a section of those in the members' reserve should have so far transgressed the unwritten laws of good sportsmanship. The whole demonstration, it should be added, was against the umpire and not against the visitors.

It is a pity that a cricketing public which was able to display such splendid appreciation of England's grand cricket on Monday should have its reputation besmirched by treatment of this kind to an umpire – who, after all, is an Australian.

Hill had played very soundly, yet more quietly than usual, for his 51. He was thoroughly set. His cricket and that of Trumper had quite revived the hopes of Australia and the disappointment arising from his dismissal in this way was beyond expression. Twenty runs had been got from the over. 4–254.

J. C. Davis would have been sitting in the grandstand that houses the players, possibly the worst spot on the ground to judge a run-out at the Randwick end of the ground. In fact, as he says, the umpire is the best man in the position to tell what is going on. And what had gone on in that over and before in the matter of sharp run-stealing hadn't put many spectators in the right frame of mind to accept a run-out of one of their heroes, especially as Australia was making a wonderful fight-back.

Clamouring thousands kept up an incessant chant of 'Crock, Crock, Crock'. Somebody on the Hill wanted to know if Crockett would stand for the Senate, in the elections then about to take place, and at the end of the day, though he was considered by everybody to be a very good umpire, he had to be escorted to a side exit by the police, as violence to him was anticipated. Plum Warner took strong exception to a piece written for the London *Mail* by Frank Iredale, who said Warner exacerbated feelings by going towards the Members' Reserve. Warner said he was merely going to plead with them, but as Noble the Australian skipper was next man in he pacified Warner, who was on the verge of leading his men off the field. 'All I intended to do', wrote Warner, 'was to appeal to the better feelings of the members, and if they had allowed me to

8. Trumper drives during the third Test at Headingley, Leeds, 1905. He made only 8 and O in this drawn match.

9. Trumper, in sun hat, cuts England's fast-medium, left arm bowler Frank Foster for 4 during the fourth Test, Melbourne, 1911-12.

12

11

10

17

Outstanding photographs from the technical study on Trumper by Fry and Beldham, 1905. 10. (plate VII) The pull. 11. (plate IX) The off drive. 12. (plate XI) The straight drive. 13. (plate XI) The follow-through. 14. (plate XV) The pull drive. 15 and 16. (plates XIX and XX) The late cut. 17. (plate XXII) The late cut, as seen from behind the stumps.

18. Trumper acknowledges the ovation with which he was greeted on going out to bat in his Testimonial match in February 1913. The game, held in Sydney between New South Wales and a Rest of Australia XI, raised over £3,000

19. Trumper's 'dog-shot'. Although he employed it often it is noticeably absent from any of the formal books on batting in which his photograph appears.

do so I feel sure I would have succeeded in persuading them to stop the demonstration against Crockett.'

Warner says he was fielding at deep mid-on to Braund when the incident happened so was not in a position to say whether the decision was correct or not : but Foster, who was standing at short-leg, and Hayward, who was at deep point, declare that Hill was out by a foot. 'But that is really besides the point,' wrote Warner. 'Crockett was there to decide such questions, and from his ruling there could be no appeal. There was absolutely no excuse for this demonstration, which was as disgraceful as it was unwarranted. It was started, as I have said, in the Members' Pavilion, from which point it was impossible to see what occurred.'

I never asked Hill about the incident, but I was told by somebody in a position to know that Hill later admitted, 'Perhaps I *was* out, by a foot or so; but it was a close thing.' The English Test umpire Charlie Elliott told me once that of all decisions a run-out is the hardest to give. Maybe both umpires should confer on a run-out, when necessary. The umpire not immediately concerned in the decision could watch to see if the ball is taken properly, if the wicket is broken with the ball in hand, if the wicket is not broken first by a foot or a body, and then, after a meeting in the middle of the pitch, the main umpire concerned, after giving his sole attention to the bat and the batsman, could give his decision.

But to return to that tumultuous day. Warner says how hard the violent atmosphere was on his bowlers, but I should have thought that it was hardest of all on Trumper. Warner gives him the highest praise :

After tea Trumper played in the most brilliant fashion. Rhodes, with three men in the country, a long-on, a long-off, and a deep extra cover, kept him fairly quiet, but everyone else who went on was roughly handled. The great batsman was playing in his own inimitable style, and scoring with splendid freedom and power all round the wicket. Every stroke was in evidence : the cut, the drive, the leg-glance; and that special one of Trumper's when he goes right back

almost on to his wicket and forces the ball just short of
a good length away past mid-on or between the off-side
fielders. Rhodes continued to bowl well, but it was Bosanquet
who got Noble stumped. At stumps the score was 367 for
five wickets, Trumper not out 119 and Armstrong not out 14.
In the hour and 40 minutes after tea Trumper made 112
runs, 64 of them in the last 40 minutes.

There were great reactions in England and Australia to that
crowd scene. A rather pompous, popinjay Governor of South
Australia read Australians in general a homily on good
manners, but I should think many of them realized they had
acted in bad taste. And there was no doubting, as both Davis
and Warner wrote, that it all began in the Members' Pavilion.
Good behaviour is not the prerogative of crowds in any cricket
land. They can all behave well or badly at times, though I fear
the practice of taking copious amounts of beer into the
Australian outer has a bad effect on many spectators, who
behave in a coarse and crude manner.

Trumper had the worst of the demonstration that afternoon.
He must have found it hard to concentrate amid all that bedlam
and so, too, I think modern batsmen must find it very hard in
a Test when the crowd, yelling for gore, want more and more
violent bowling. Test batsmen are entitled to silence while the
bowler is running in. His job is hard enough, especially in
modern days when the fast bowler is allowed so much latitude
with bouncers – far too much, I might add. But to continue
Warner's report:

The magnificent fight Australia were making brought over
20,000 people to the ground on the fifth day of the match.
Everything depended on whether the remaining batsmen
would stay with Trumper. Did they do so, we might be set
an almost impossible task for a fourth innings on a worn
pitch. But Rhodes came to the rescue, as he has so often
done before for England and Yorkshire; and though Trumper
remained unshaken his companions did not lend him any

very great assistance. There had been a little rain during the night, which served to bind the wicket together. Rhodes soon had Armstrong caught at slip and, after Hirst had relieved him for a few overs after the 400 had gone up, he tempted Hopkins to hit into cover's hands. While Trumper and Hopkins were together the Australians had a good chance of ultimate victory, for every moment the wicket was becoming more worn, as any wicket is bound to do on which 1300 runs had been made. After lunch the game took a sudden turn in our favour, Laver being easily caught at slip, Howell finely taken at the wicket and Saunders run out. Trumper was left undefeated. He gave nothing like a chance, and was Trumper at his best. Of Rhodes's bowling during that long innings I cannot speak too highly; he was our tower of strength in the day of battle.

Australians who saw that innings say it was the best of all Trumper's great innings. He got 185 not out, outshining even the brilliant Foster. Carter raved about it, yet it was to be followed by the best innings, many declare, that was ever played on a 'sticky' pitch.

A 'sticky' pitch in Melbourne has to be known to be believed. Johnny Tyldesley, 62 out of an England total of 103, played grandly on that pitch, but Warner says the pitch was a 'real beast' when the Australians went in and they should have been out for less than 122, and so made to follow on. 'But the follow-on was saved by a mighty effort by Trumper, who went in first and was last out, caught at long-off. It was a grand achievement on a bowler's wicket; but he was very lucky, being missed four times. Three of the chances were off the bowling of Rhodes, at 3, over 50, and by me at 64. However, a batsman must have luck on a "sticky" – and a Melbourne one at that, when the ball off a good length flies round his face with devilish speed and turn.'

After that Test the ubiquitous Charles Fry was at a London dinner and in a moment of inspiration sprang to his feet, glass in hand: 'Gentlemen, I give you a toast. It is to Victor

Trumper, first in, last out, 74 runs out of a total of 122, on a vile pitch and against the best bad-pitch bowlers in the world.' A nice tribute.

That was a series of grand cricket. In the third Test, in Adelaide, Trumper made 113, his third century in five Tests, and he made a quick 59 in the second innings. He made only seven and twelve in the return Sydney Test, and a splendid 88 in one hour 50 minutes in Melbourne, to finish the series with a duck, bowled by Hirst in Melbourne. For that Melbourne Test, Trumble returned to Test cricket to play his last Test and, fittingly for such a big figure in cricket in every way, finished his career with a hat-trick with the wickets of Bosanquet, Warner and Lilley.

Two interesting facts emerge from that series from the Australian viewpoint. First, Noble did not impress with his captaincy, Joe Darling being asked back to take the 1905 team to England; and secondly, despite all the uproar over the Hill run-out in Sydney, Bob Crockett was asked to stand in all five Tests. Somebody must have been satisfied with his umpiring – although the NSW Cricket Association queried the amount of £10 which he charged, very modestly, I think, for his services, travelling and general expenses. The fee charged by Crockett was the one English umpires charged at that time. The NSWCA laid it down that if Warner wanted any particular umpire in the future – it appears he was impressed by Crockett's ability – and he had to travel, he would be paid £1 and all expenses. Poor old Crockett got little enough for all that abuse he had to withstand in Sydney. And that notwithstanding the gate money, £4274 10s, all taken at the turnstiles, which was then a Test record.

9

The Commerce of Cricket

In 1976, Jeff Thomson, the Australian fast bowler, has signed a ten-year contract for 63,000 dollars a year with a Brisbane broadcasting firm. The figures make one's eyes boggle. It is more money than the Prime Minister is paid. I had the great pleasure of doing a television interview with Jeff after the Test series against the West Indies had finished – finished in acute disappointment I might add, because after promising so much (they wiped the floor with Australia in Perth) they fell away into mediocrity.

But Victor Trumper has nothing to do with this. In Trumper's time the West Indies were known for the pirates who used to do their deeds there, not for cricket. But it is interesting to compare Trumper's financial experiences with those of Thomson. Trumper went into the sports-goods business in Sydney with three men – Dodge, Hanson Carter and J. J. Giltinan, one of the founders of the Rugby League code in Australia. All three businesses failed, ostensibly because Trumper was such a poor businessman.

Today, the first man to attach himself to Trumper would be an agent – or, as they are known, a 'ten percenter', since he receives ten per cent of all money made. Trumper would have had his by-line on articles, not necessarily written by himself, and he would have had his name on bats, for royalties. (I got Jeff Thomson to admit that possibly he had been wrongly presented to the public as a 'killer', a fast bowler who would rather see a batsman spitting blood on the pitch than see his stumps cartwheeling. I didn't see Thomson in this light, no matter what opposing batsmen might have thought of him. I found him a very friendly man – co-operative, and with much more intelligence than some in the Press-box were apt

to concede to him.) The agent, then, would have stuck to
Trumper like a limpet and made a good businessman out of
him. How co-operative Trumper would have been is conjec-
tural. He seldom used gloves (though pictures of him show him
with two on), but he would have been jockeyed into using
'Vic Trumper' gloves, pads with his name on them (he so often
used a poor type of pad, with thin cane ribbing) and all the
other personal items that the modern cricketer wears. Ian
Chappell once told me that he had been rummaging in grandfather Vic Richardson's old cricket bag and came up with some
odd pieces of protection. I knew immediately what he meant
and I think Ian had a poor opinion of batsmen who would go
out to bat with a thin piece of crepe rubber, covered with
white cloth, under their cricket shirts. 'Somebody gave us all
one of them,' I told Ian, 'but as you can guess from seeing
them they weren't worth a cracker. They were more bother
than worth, and most of us didn't use them after a while.'
But such a gimmick would have been snaffled by the man I
imagine would have been Vic Trumper's agent and, with his
name on them for royalties, would have become common wear
for batsmen in all grades of cricket. Trumper had no fads or
fancies about his bat. I saw two of them in New Zealand and
one in the Long Room at Lord's, in a cabinet along with those
of many other famous cricketers, and he certainly didn't have
an autographed bat as Don Bradman did and many, many
others. Nowadays, to catch a glimpse through the camera,
players have all manner of odd creations running up and down
the back of the bat. But so far Lord's has stood out against
the coloured bat for colour television.

Bill Mandle has given us an excellent insight into the development of the finances of the game in both Australia and England.
The sharp brains in various teams were well known for their
business dealings during a tour, and there is plenty of evidence
to show how the earlier Englishmen helped themselves in selling cricket kits and bats, and buying jewellery and nuggets of
gold to take home. Many of the Australian teams in England
got themselves disliked for their rapacity in setting up for
themselves what were commonly known in the side as

'gimmees' – free presents – and many a player got incredible amounts of cricketing goods past the Customs to be sold for a good sum to the local player who wanted to look his best in English cricketing cloth or who wished to use the best English bats and pads. When our team arrived in London in 1938 a chap from a London newspaper sidled up to me and said, 'I believe you are a journalist. I have a proposition to make to you. If you keep us informed of what is going on behind the scenes [the so-called 'dressing-room stories'] we will pay you so much at the end of the tour.' And he mentioned a big sum for those days. I told him there was nothing doing, that we each signed a contract with our Board that we wouldn't talk or give information to the Press. He replied, 'You do live in a make-believe world. Why, so-and-so has done this job for us for tour after tour,' as if I were the biggest sucker he had ever met. Maybe I was, but cricket is in many ways like politics. If you keep your eyes open and read between the lines of approval or disapproval of certain individuals or players, you can usually work out who is 'leaking'. We worked out one such in South Africa and maybe this London pressman got somebody else who was willing to aid him. I often wondered as I read various descriptions of games.

But Trumper, in this modern age, would never have been allowed to be the bad businessman he was because of his unbusinesslike generosity. What the agent would have done about his favourite beverage (he was a strict tee-totaller) and his favourite brand of cigarette (he never smoked) I don't know, but something would have been wangled. The cricketers of the nineteenth century in both Australia and England often finished in the poor-house. Mandle says in *The Professional Cricketer in England in the Nineteenth Century* that even in the eighteenth century cricket was flourishing in the South of England. Aristocrats such as the Dukes of Dorset, Newcastle, Hamilton and Richmond, the Earls of Winchilsea and Sandwich and Lords Tankerville and Beauclerk gathered teams together, nominally called Kent, Sussex or Surrey, to play games for stakes and satisfaction. At this stage there were 'professionals' of a sort, employees on the estates of the gentry who played, as 'Silver Billy' Beldham said, 'if Master allows the time' – or, if they were one of cricket's early champions, such as 'Lumpy' Stevens, when Lord Tankerville, who employed him as a gardener, wanted a match played and won. Strictly speaking, as Mandle says, these men were not professional cricketers, but in class and function they were the prototype of the nineteenth-century version. They played under the orders and at the behest of their social superiors, the equivalents of the amateurs who organized, ran and captained the county and representative sides of a century later.

There was, however, a strange interlude when the professional cricketer might fashion his own game, run by professionals for professionals. After a lull occasioned by the Napoleonic wars, the game began to pick up again in the 1830s and gentlemen in charge of county clubs began to pay good cricketers to settle in their districts and play. Fuller Pilch, the Dr Grace of the early part of the century, was given £100 a year to live in Kent from 1835. Charles Dickens ran his own team on his own ground and had a love for the game, as he showed in his account of the Dingley Dell match in *Pickwick Papers*.

From the 1840s on the railways encouraged travel and competition, and amateur club sides were founded solely for the purpose of touring, I Zingari being outstanding. There were by now enough professional cricketers to follow suit and, in September 1846, William Clarke, a one-eyed Nottingham bowler and publican, brought together what he called an All England Eleven to play Twenty of Sheffield. The game was a success, and for the next 25 years the All England Eleven and its imitators and rivals toured the country playing Eighteens and Twenty-twos wherever a ground could be prepared and a gate collected. Clarke paid each of his men £4 a match and took the balance of the takings for himself. His meanness and the realization that a market for cricket was there caused splits, secessions, and new creations in the professional ranks.

It was in combination, however, that English professional teams undertook the first overseas tours, to America and

Canada (unlikely cricket countries) in 1859, and to Australia in 1861 and 1863. But the future of cricket in England did not lie with the professional touring sides. Their very success encouraged the growth of local cricket, and the wholesale adoption of the game by the public schools helped to revive county cricket. The middle classes and the aristocracy re-asserted their control of the game. They provided jobs as coaches and ground bowlers, invested in cricket arenas and formed and re-formed county clubs. In 1840 only 15 county clubs were in existence; by 1860 there were 25, and by 1870 there were 34. The professional cricketer's bid for independence had failed, but the new structure of cricket gave him increasing opportunities, albeit of a different nature.

The boom in cricket, spreading to second-class counties, benefited the professionals. In 1872 there were 79 professionals; in 1896 there were 180. The proliferation of school and club coaching jobs, of ground-staff bowling positions, and, even later in the century, of overseas coaching appointments in Australia, South Africa and America, added to the growing list of opportunities for the professional cricketer. As to which strata of society these professionals came, Mandle says that in 1862 fourteen were engaged in agriculture, seventeen in trade or shopkeeping, fourteen in clothing or textile manufacture, 22 were craftsmen or in light industry, two were clerks and there was one college servant and one coachman.

The professional cricketer, therefore, was demonstrably of the working class, but equally demonstrably of a slightly superior section of it, in that most of the men listed had a trade, or a shop – even in the rare instance a profession.

Alfred Shaw the Notts bowler says in his ghosted reminiscences that the hand-loom weavers in the small Notts town where he was born 'worked when they liked and played when they had a mind to'. Paid at piece-work rates they could choose when and how hard they worked; consequently many of them used the hours of darkness to weave and the hours of daylight to play. Notts towns such as Sutton, Burton Joyce, Hucknall and Radcliffe-on-Trent were the great professional nurseries. Farther north, Yorkshire towns with communities

I

of weavers provided similar supplies of cricketers. Lascelles Hall, a small town near Huddersfield, was famous for its weavers and cricketers.

The periodical [*Bell's Life*] of July 1871 noted with accuracy the reason for the flood of cricketers from villages:

> An agricultural district cannot produce them; the farm labourer is too unwieldy, too stiff in his joints, too slow in expedients for that nice combination of hand and head necessary for success with the ball. On the other hand, a large town cannot produce them, because the bowler should be a man of excellent physique, and, besides, have the opportunity of unremitting practice till his bowling becomes, so to speak, mechanism tempered with intellect. Moreover, the dwellers in a city, for the most part, have settled occupations which they cannot take up or put down at pleasure. The true nursery of professional bowlers is the country village which is the seat of a flourishing manufacturing industry, and which is also near some larger town, where the excitement, the encouragement, and the harsh criticism of large bodies of spectators may be had. Nottingham abounds with such villages, and so does Yorkshire. Leicestershire, with her prosperous hamlets inhabited by stocking-weavers, ought to be a rare breeding ground for bowlers; and the very creditable appearance made by Middlesex's team at Lord's suggests that the present executive is becoming alive to its opportunities. Unless a young man has a trade to fall back upon and unless he has a cricket ground at his back door, he will be elbowed out in the race of cricket competition.

Interestingly, a very small number of cricketers were born in Lancashire, possibly a reflection of the comparatively highly industrialized nature of the county. By and large, the professional cricketer came from a town or village, not from the city, and rarely from the factory.

By the standards of the time, the earnings of the professional cricketer were not at all bad. The difficulty was that employment was limited to the summer months and within them to individual matches. In the 1860s the Surrey professional was paid £3 a match plus a £1 win bonus. By the 1870s the basic rate was £5 a match with the MCC paying £1 travel allowance for trips over one hundred miles. Match fees were higher for more important games: £10 for Players v. Gentlemen and £6 for North v. South. These fees improved towards the end of the century, an MCC player getting up to £7 for an away match, and from £10 to £30 for a representative game.

Salaries did not come in until the twentieth century and in those earlier days the ordinary professional cricketer could expect to make £80 or so for a five months' season, with a first-class professional perhaps doubling that figure. The average unskilled labourer at this time would be paid about £85 per annum. The last decade of the century saw this situation improve, until by 1900 the professional's salary of some £275 per annum compared more than favourably with a labourer's wage of £95.

The professional's fees were rarely obtained from match fees. Coaching and ground-staff positions were readily available from the 1840s on. These positions fell into six categories. First were the engagements at the Marylebone (Lord's) and the Oval. There were ten engaged at Lord's in 1844, 40 by 1891. They had match fees if they played but had a basic rate for bowling to members of from 30/- to 50/- a week. (We would often use these professional bowlers, members of the ground staff, if we wanted a net at Lord's. They had to be tipped.)

There were coaching posts at the Universities, and in 1878 no fewer than 25 professionals were engaged to bowl to the undergraduates at various colleges at Oxford. In earlier days Caffyn had been a pro at Christ Church, being paid £1 a week and 1/6 an hour. The young gentlemen's habit of putting a shilling on the stumps for the pro to disturb them and grab it boosted this 1/6 to 18/- an hour, Caffyn laconically said. At Fenner's, Cambridge, the regular pros were augmented by 'seedy-looking' men who offered to bowl for 1/- an hour as late as the 1880s.

The public schools were increasingly ready to hire professional cricketers as coaches. Neville Cardus writes entrancingly of the time he spent at Shrewsbury College as a cricket coach, though Neville, his memory will forgive me saying, was but a very ordinary cricketer. He was at his best with his brolly in the Mound stand at Lord's where, in emulation of MacLaren particularly, he invariably got centuries between breaks.

W. H. Luck, the Kent cricketer, coached at Tonbridge and ran also a tuck-shop and pub at the same time. The influence of the pro, however, was not always highly regarded. Edward Lyttelton wrote:

> Certain it is that a professional bowler engaged by a school, if he be a man of good manners and willing to speak dogmatically, will have a strange influence over young cricketers, which would be very absurd were it not somewhat injurious. Not only cricket, but many matters, some of them tinged with the associations of low life, will the boys look at through the professional's eyes, and it seems undesirable that this functionary should be invested with an even larger influence than the possession of a peculiar gift and of strong, though ill-balanced, opinions will inevitably secure for him.

Finally, the professional could be employed privately by an individual anxious to improve his own or his son's cricket, or to put a team in the field rather in the eighteenth-century manner. The highest in the land did not scorn the use of a pro cricketer. F. W. Bell was employed to bowl at the royal princes at Windsor in the 1880s. He remarked that he 'couldn't make a job of them at all'. The greatest of the private employers was Lord Sheffield, a Sussex magnate who took upon himself the task of reviving Sussex cricket in the 1880s and hired Shaw and Mycroft to find and coach young talent. Mycroft died of consumption but Shaw became a constant companion of the peer, travelling everywhere with him. Lord Sheffield brought a team to Australia in 1891–2 at a personal loss of £2000 on the tour. He presented the Sheffield Shield, which is still Australia's foremost cricket competition.

As cricket spread throughout the world opportunities arose for overseas coaching. To the United States went Butler, Lane, McIntyre and Morley. McIntyre was paid £5 a week by the Philadelphia club in 1869 and given a benefit match. Atfield, Bean, Briggs and F. Hearne were among those who went to South Africa, Atfield being hired by Sir Abe Bailey, then staying on to coach in Johannesburg and Durban. Johnny Briggs, the somewhat eccentric Lancashire bowler, was offered £300 to coach in South Africa during the English winter. There was also some professional traffic to Australia and India.

More lucrative rewards from overseas came to those engaged in tours, especially to Australia. For professionals lucky or brave enough (the prospect of the voyage deterred many in 1860) to make the trip, the profits were, in contemporary terms, enormous. The 1861–2 trip to Australia gained each man £250 plus a first-class passage home. Even greater killings were made by the 1863–4 tourist who, in addition to profits of £475 a man, took home 'sufficient jewellery to stock a small shop', and in Oscroft's case the profits from cricket gear he had foresightedly brought out with him to sell. 'I went out to Australia to make as much money as I could,' he recalled. But the money-grubbing of this side helped to delay further tours until 1873, though later regular trips always brought profits to the promoters and the professionals. Bobby Abel on the 1894–5 tour stuck out for £500 to make the trip; he didn't get it, so did not come.

There were other perks in the way of a cheque or a piece of silver for an outstanding performance. Caffyn, who seemed to be the most peripatetic cricketer of his time, once backed himself to play the whole Winchester first XI and win. He did. He made 35 and one, Winchester, the acme of consistency, four and four.

On retirement the luckier cricketers could expect a benefit match with which they might set themselves up in a sports outfitter's shop, a pub or a tobacconist shop (it was in one such that I came across Harold Larwood in Blackpool in 1948, though he did not even have his name over the door). Despite all this, there was much hardship for the professional cricketer.

It was only the fortunate minority that commanded lucrative fees, coaching positions, 'perks', presentations and overseas trips; and even they expressed on occasions dissatisfaction with their lot. Seven Notts pros went on strike in 1881, and in 1896 five English players 'struck' before the Test with Australia. In 1855, Julius Caeser (*sic*) and H. H. Stephenson refused to play for Surrey unless they got a pay increase, and they stood down all the summer when it was refused.

The profits being made by the so-called 'amateur' Australian touring teams incensed the English professional, who saw the Australians lionized, generally made much of (always called 'Mr') and treated as gentlemen while the Englishman, poor devil, had to touch his hat to 'my lord' or a gentleman player. In September 1880 seven Notts players demanded £20 a man to play against the Australians. The Notts committee bowed to *force majeure* but spitefully paid £21 to the professionals who 'knew their place'.

The Big Strike happened in 1896, on the eve of the third Test against Australia at the Oval, when Lohmann, Abel, Hayward, Richardson and W. Gunn demanded £20 as their match fee instead of the customary £10; but all except Gunn and Lohmann capitulated, and later Lohmann apologized. The exaggerated 'expenses' given to so-called amateurs, together with the profits being made by Surrey and the Australians out of the Test, were given as reasons for the strike. To a great extent the professionals seemed, or had to be, content with their lot.

The professional's working-class origin was, particularly in the middle years of the century, betrayed by his manners. He also laboured under burdens of financial hardship. Out of his match fee he had to pay for his accommodation and meals; lunch was not provided until late in the century, and he had to find his own bed. If he wished to save his fee he could, as one Notts professional did, sleep out of doors in his cricket flannels. Often he had only one set of cricket clothes, so he became noted for 'rather dirty white flannels'. Walter Hearne describes his life in the 1880s: 'I had to get wickets ready, to puts nets up, to bowl from two o'clock until five, with a rest of half an hour for tea, and then bowl again until it was dark – sometimes until nine o'clock. I also had to make the wicket and then go on to bowl.' One hopes at least Hearne made a few wickets to suit his style of bowling.

Hard work and the pressing necessity to do well encouraged caution in the professional cricketer. Not for him the flashing bat of the amateur; he became noted for 'a certain way of plodding on with dogged determination'. But gradually his image improved. Lyttelton remarked how the professional around the 1900s was better dressed, better educated and in better trim than his predecessors. Whereas a professional would often spend his lunch hour at the bar, accompanied by his admirers and hangers-on, the amateur was provided with proper eating facilities. But the pro became respectable. Much of the improvement in his conditions was due to Lord Hawke, who introduced systematic talent schemes, winter pay, investment of benefits and travel allowances to his side in the 1890s. He also undertook a moral crusade against the waywardness of the professional cricketer whose life-style only too often included partiality for the drinks he was offered by so many well-meaning admirers during his lunch break. The Yorkshire team was particularly notorious for its addiction to alcohol – 'an eleven of ten drunks and a parson', they were often called. Lord Hawke changed all that; but he had one spectacular failure in 1897 when Peel, his England bowler, in a state of some distress, first aimed a trial ball at the sight-screen behind him and then 'watered the pitch in an unorthodox fashion'. Peel never played for Yorkshire again. He was a publican, and a notable feature of professional cricketers was the number of them who ran pubs and the number of them who died while landlords, often quite young, from diseases of the kidney or liver.

As deadly as drink were the hazards of cold and wet conditions. Lord Harris, captain of Kent and well disposed towards professionals, wrote:

And we should not forget that the spring and autumn work of cricket is hard on the professional. The grass is often wet

and he has not his patron's array of boots and shoes to fall
back on. Also he becomes very hot with his exertion of
bowling and has not a servant as we have to bring us an
overcoat when we sit down to luncheon after an easy
morning's shooting. Consequently, pulmonary disease often
attacks the professional cricketer, who rarely makes old
bones.

Mandle himself found thirteen such cricketers who died of
consumption, the oldest 47, the majority in their thirties.
Another three died of cold and wet, another of rheumatism.
For many death came with the player destitute or his family
unprovided for. George Davidson of Derbyshire died in 1899,
aged 32, leaving six children under the age of seven and no
money. Some were always on the threshold of the workhouse
or suicide. John Jackson of Notts, 'a bent and grisly old man of
67', existed on a pittance of 5/6 weekly paid him out of a
Cricketers' Fund set up by prominent professionals in 1862. As
with most of Britain's work-force the professional cricketer had
to await proper social services before he could know security.
It is only fair to add that the picture is at least one of
gradually relieving gloom. By the turn of the century the
professional cricketer was becoming less of a second-class
citizen. There might be three bathrooms installed for amateur
cricketers at Old Trafford, but in Yorkshire separate dressing-
rooms were abolished, again by Lord Hawke. Amateurs might
argue that the professionals liked to live apart, but there was
increasing reliance on the advice and skill of the professional.
As for life-style, one has only to look at photographs of teams
at the turn of the century and compare them with those from
the 1860s. This description by Rogerson of Wilfred Rhodes in
a railway-carriage just after the turn of the century exemplifies
the change even more clearly :

He was wearing a well-cut grey flannel suit. His brown shoes
shone with much polishing and his straw hat had the scarlet
and yellow band of MCC – or else he was wearing an MCC
tie, I forget which. With his deeply-tanned face he looked,

I remember thinking, almost exactly like the young captain in the 60th Rifles who used when on leave from India to attend the parish church at Pateley Bridge.

By the turn of the century Jack Hobbs could state that his favourite drinks were milk, tea and ginger beer, 'but a real good brand is hard to get', and Fred Root could claim that schoolboy cricketers were far and away better book learners than their non-playing fellows. The coming of salaries, contracts, better education and a growing pride in an increasingly skilful craft helped to transform the nineteenth-century professional cricketer.

Mandle adds that not all professional cricketers finished their career on the breadline. George Parr lived into a prosperous old age and William Gunn, maker of the best bat I knew in my time and used by most Test players, the 'Star' Autograph, died worth £60,000. He might also have added that professional cricketers like Jack Hobbs and Len Hutton were knighted and that Hammond, reverting to amateurism, Hutton, Illingworth and Greig, all professionals, captained England in Test matches. But then amateurism died as such in the 1960s and today all cricketers in England are equal.

I would think, too, that cricketers of today are much better businessmen than their predecessors. They rarely let a chance slide these days and insist on their pound of flesh. Tony Greig, the former English captain, is a case in point. He came in 1975–6 to Australia, ostensibly to play with my old club, Waverley, in Sydney grade cricket. He filled in the other moments by putting his name to articles, televising and broadcasting, and pushing his own brand of cricket gear. I would think he made one of the biggest 'killings' of all cricket time – so big that he spoke at the beginning of the English summer of not being available to tour India with England but of coming back to Waverley. He should have known that he could never strike another Indian summer like that. And to think that Alan Kippax, whose bootlaces I respectfully submit Greig wasn't fit to tie as a batsman, had to pay 2/- every Saturday with Waverley, for ground and scoring fees!

10

Trumper against the Googly

The South Africans visited Australia in 1910–11. South Africa had gone 'googly' crazy, it seemed, and for their first tour of Australia relied almost completely on off-spin bowled with a leg-break action. Trumper and Duff were at home immediately against the new-fangled ball. It seemed that batsmen like Armstrong and Macartney were at sea at first, but they later followed the tactics of Trumper, Duff, Hill, Bardsley and company and used their feet to get down the wicket to the slows. Trumper had a good look at Schwarz, the South Africans' star bowler, and he was careful to master his googlies, for he could bowl nothing else. The *Telegraph* correspondent, who seems to have been a reliable judge of the game, said of Trumper's 74 runs in 94 minutes scored in the match between the South Africans and NSW, 'He was not the brilliant Trumper, but a batsman of the solid, conventional order. It was not an exhibition of Trumper but it was a good batting exposition, none the less.'

The correspondent noted that Faulkner clean-bowled E. F. Waddy, a member of a talented Sydney cricketing family, who was waiting with his bat poised for a leg-break but the ball came straight through. Faulkner got 5–40 in that innings and the Sydney crowd, well prepared for the bowling mysteries of the Springboks, were saying of this ball during the luncheon break, 'It was a googly. It broke a foot.' Nothing of the sort, said the correspondent: it was a straight ball that didn't break. Trumper gave them stick in the second innings, in which he got another 70. The *Telegraph* correspondent commented:

Our visitors were unfortunate in that they met Trumper at

his best. That generally means that the opposition loses its head. This was not so with the South Africans. They set NSW 212 to win and Trumper and Duff looked like getting that themselves. But every man on the South African side was a trier, and although it seemed they were in for a hiding they stuck to their task. The bowlers threw them up only to see the ball cracked to the fence time and time again. The South Africans saw the figures on the board mount like a sky rocket. Ten upon ten followed in quick succession. Trumper was playing a tune against the fence. Fifty runs came in half as many minutes. It seemed that men were belting children. The children went on impervious to lyddite, shrapnel and rifle fire but they hit back by bagging the biggest gun of the NSW side. Then they bagged some more. And shortly before time they added six more scalps to their belt.

Trumper was eventually stumped by Sherwell off Faulkner for 78 at better than a run a minute, and so captivated were the tourists by his batting that they joined in the ovation on his way to the pavilion.

In the Test, Schwarz bowled the first maiden over to the Australians only after 87 overs had been bowled. The South Africans bowled 109.4 overs and in all used seven bowlers. Trumper, Hill, Bardsley and Gehrs made Schwarz look very simple, but against Armstrong, Ransford and Macartney he looked a champion and tied them in knots. Australia made 494–6 that first day, but some weren't pleased. 'A section of the crowd on the Outer,' it was reported, 'stamped their feet, whistled, hooted and generally behaved as if they had left their manners at home.'

The tourists' dependence on spin was amplified when Llewellyn, some six feet tall, came on first change and rubbed the new ball in the dirt to get a better spinning grip. Ramadhin once did that in Brisbane. There would be a revolution these days of rubbing, licking and polishing on the seat of the pants if anybody did that now – to put a sheen back on the ball!

It was said that Schwarz would have been a world-beater if he could bowl a leg-break. He obviously lost it when learning to bowl the googly. So useless did the South Africans consider the new ball that they began the match with only one slip. Pearse, who did not bowl at home, was given a trial and got the wickets of Bardsley, Hill and Gehrs, Bardsley falling to a ball that a schoolboy would have smacked for four. The Australians got 400 in 214 minutes and it was a boon for the visitors that Trumper was run out for 27.

But Schwarz had made a good impression. One critic said the Australians knew nothing of googly bowling (they seemed to learn fast) and it was said that Schwarz was the bosie's greatest exponent of this ball in the cricketing world. 'He has out-bosied Bosanquet.' I also like this phrase of the *Telegraph* man in Melbourne written after Faulkner had made 204 in 315 minutes : 'He made the iron spikes of the boundary fence ring like a tuning fork.'

In the second Test Trumper came back with a century in 117 minutes. Nobody knows whether Trumper should have been in the pavilion early. Sherwell believed he had caught him when he had made only a few runs, but the umpire ruled against him. Afterwards the champion batted in splendid style, reminiscent of the time when he was without peer. His innings of 159 put his side back with a chance. Schwarz got the wickets of Hill, Bardsley, Gehrs and Ransford for 50 runs. Trumper hit one six and 15 fours. South Africa, making 506 against 348, wanted only 170 to win but (again the *Telegraph* man) : 'South Africa had built up their edifice of victory and had only to place the coping stone on it to complete the job, but the scaffolding collapsed and the whole lot tumbled around their ears.' They could manage only 80, but there were some compensations. Silver-mounted balls were presented to Nourse and Commaille as mementoes of fine catches and a golden-bat emblem was given to Faulkner for his fine double century.

Trumper's greatest innings against them was just ahead at Adelaide, where he hit 214 not out, of 354 made in 242 minutes, where the weather was so humid that the Adelaide house-fly 'creepy and crawly and with feet of glue' worried all the players on the field. By Adelaide, too, the visitors were showing injuries, many of them caused by Tibby Cotter's fast bowling. 'Many of them are more injured than many soldiers in the twelve months' campaign of the Boer War.' Llewellyn was very sore with some ugly bruises on his thigh.

Despite the heat and the flies, Trumper was 208 not out at stumps.

He made a slow start but suddenly woke up to bat brilliantly and scored at a great rate. In former years, he was inclined to recklessness especially after he had made a century. That usually was a sign for wild hitting until someone brought off a catch near the boundary. For some time today he was just as careful after making 100 as if he had not made a run and never took the slightest risk and never gave a chance. He was, perhaps, more conventional than usual. He did not pull a ball unless it was short. Anything he could hit on the forward movement was driven.

The pitch was like a loaf of bread, 'crisp on the top and soft underneath'. Snooke and Nourse opened the bowling though neither was as fast as Noble. Sherwell stood back to make them look fast. Trumper was sure on the leg side and he made some lovely cuts. Only on a few occasions did he follow the ball play and late-cut it. He was always safe. He scored with superlative ease off balls that kept other batsmen quiet. No one else on the side could manage more than 54. The three-figure innings of Snooke and Zulch paled into insignificance compared with this exhibition.

11

The 'Big Six' Upheaval

A year of great importance in Trumper's life was 1912, when he stood firm with his fellows, Armstrong, Hill, Ransford, Carter and Cotter, and refused to accept an invitation from the Board of Control to travel to England to play the first and only Triangular Tournament between England, South Africa and Australia. That team was led by Syd Gregory, then well past his best, and included Macartney and Bardsley; but the venture was a rank failure and the tournament has never been repeated.

The 1912 dispute rent Australian cricket from top to bottom. There were incidents, public meetings, fist-fights and bitter disruptions of friendships, and the row welled over into the columns of newspapers. I will try to give a précis of it, based largely on the details given in D. K. Darling's book about his father, the Hon. Joe Darling, CBE, MLC, *Test Tussles on and off the Field*.

Joe Darling's 1905 side to England was the last Australian team to tour England under the system of the players appointing their own manager and captain and managing their own affairs. Naturally, such a state of affairs could not persist, and in 1905 the Board of Control was formed. Darling was a delegate, and when the constitution was drawn up he had Rule 9 inserted which said: 'The players of all future Australian teams to England or elsewhere appoint their own manager, subject to the approval of the Board only.' The Board demurred, however, when the players wanted Frank Laver as manager of the 1912 tour. Darling said that Laver had proved his ability as a player and manager during the 1905 and 1909 tours, that the players had implicit confidence in him, and that he was held in high esteem in cricketing circles in England. I heard that Laver's unacceptability to the Board arose when he wouldn't submit certain financial details of a tour to them; but Darling says it was mainly because he sided with the players over the trouble which arose between the Melbourne Cricket Club and the Victorian Cricket Association when the Board was partly formed. Darling had a row with McElhone over the visit of a Fiji team to Australia and Darling charged that the minutes were 'faked'.

Darling held that the Melbourne Cricket Club did much to foster the game in Australia, financing Australian teams to England and English teams out here. He says at one stage that the VCA was so short of funds that it cancelled a Victorian visit to Sydney. The MCC stepped in and the team went. Victoria, NSW and Queensland were the first members of the Board. This Board sent an invitation to Marylebone in London to send out a team but that body replied that until the Board was properly representative of Australian cricket it would not send any MCC side to Australia. Darling says in the midst of a Victoria–South Australia game he called a meeting, and it was decided that if the leading NSW players were agreeable a letter would be sent to the Melbourne club, asking them to bring out a team, and they would all bind themselves to play for Australia. Darling believed this was in the best interests of Australian cricket, as the Melbourne club was the body which had financed such tours in the past and Marylebone had definitely refused the invitation of the Australian Board.

Darling claims that this letter to the Melbourne club was the cause of most of the trouble. The NSW Association disqualified all its players who had signed the letter, Hill and Darling said they would not play again in Sydney until the disqualifications were lifted – and they were lifted – and Darling claims that all the players who signed that letter to the Melbourne club were victimized later by the Board and until 1926 were not considered as selectors or managers for Australian teams. He says that all the Board business was arranged before it even met and that the reason Laver was turned down was because he had signed that letter to the Melbourne club. He also says that

Armstrong, who led the very successful 1921 side in England, only got the job on the deciding vote of the Tasmanian delegate to the Board.

There was friction on the 1909 tour with Laver as manager and Peter McAlister as treasurer. The men didn't get on; and another fact held against McAlister was that he was made vice-captain before Trumper. When G. S. Crouch, of Queensland, was appointed manager over Laver in 1912, in a letter to the Board that was very temperate in tone the six players held that the Board had acted illegally in not allowing them to choose their manager, as promised, and considered it unfair that the manager's costs should be set against the player's profits. They told Mr Syd Smith, secretary of the Board, that under those conditions they were not available.

The Melbourne *Australasian* commented:

The NSW and Queensland members of the Board of Control, assisted by Messrs Bean and Rush of Victoria, have succeeded in making an awful hash of Australian cricket. The game has been sacrificed for the sake of making players understand that the will of McElhone, Bean, Foxton and Co. is law. And all because the caucus considers it was slighted by Mr F. Laver, the last Australian manager, and that the players were at the back of Mr Laver. The demonstrations in favour of Clem Hill in Melbourne and Sydney afforded clear proof that the people who go to see Test matches are behind the players. It was made evident last Saturday that in Sydney, the stronghold of Mr McElhone, the sympathy of the public is at least divided. The cheering of the Sydney crowd for Hill proved that the Sydney papers who support Mr McElhone have not been reflecting public sympathy in the matter. Look at the way South Australia has been treated. When Hill resigned from the selection committee the SACA nominated Dr Dolling in his place, but Mr McElhone, without any meeting of the Board, appointed Mayne as selector for South Australia and the first thing Mayne did, as McAlister did in 1909, was to follow the example of McAlister and give himself a trip to England. Had Hill, Trumper and Armstrong, the interstate captains, been the selectors, they never would have thought of putting Mayne in the side.

The Melbourne paper wanted the trip abandoned but the team went, nonetheless, and the tour lost £1286. The manager, Mr Crouch, said in his report: 'Further, I would remind you that the members of the Australian XI come prominently before the eye in England, and from a national point of view it is desirable that you shall send men who will realize the responsibilities of their position and be a credit to their country.' *Wisden* also had a few words to say: 'The tour did not pass off without unpleasantness. Manager Crouch lodged a scathing complaint with the Board, stating that some of the players conducted themselves so badly in England as to lead the team to be socially ostracized. It may be added that some of the players themselves were not at all satisfied with Mr Crouch as manager.'

In this wise, then, did Victor Trumper bow out of cricket between Australia and England. Armstrong and Carter made happy returns, Ransford was to retire and become a very popular secretary of the Melbourne Cricket Club – loyalty to which club Darling puts as the base of all the trouble, but it had obviously been building up for a long time – and Clem Hill also retired. Cotter was killed at Beersheba, in Palestine.

However, before Hill bowed out he was to figure in a remarkable scene in Sydney with Peter McAlister, who was obviously a Board man. The scene was Bull's Chambers, in Martin Place, Sydney. Clem Hill was not hitting it off with his fellow Australian selectors, Iredale and McAlister. Macartney was the man over whom the storm broke. He had been brilliant against the South Africans and McAlister's ignorance of cricket may be gathered from his refusal to agree to Charlie Macartney's selection (although Melbourne had always been a bad ground for Charlie). When Hill wired McAlister from Adelaide, wanting Macartney, McAlister replied, 'If you must have Macartney, drop yourself.' As Hill was captain of the Australian Eleven and had just made 98, one of his many missed centuries in Tests, against England at Adelaide, that was a cheeky sugges-

K

tion, especially as McAlister was not even in the side.

The selectors met at Bull's Chamber to choose the final team and by that time feeling was very high between the two declared camps.

McAlister, who played in eight Tests with an average of 16 and a highest score of 41, criticized Hill's captaincy when the selectors met. It was pretty severe and Hill replied: 'The Australians wouldn't have gone to England under you.'

McAlister replied: 'I'm a better skipper than you and Trumper put together. You are the worst captain I've seen, Hill, and if you keep on insulting me I'll punch your nose.' McAlister then repeated the words, 'You are the worst captain I've ever seen.'

Hill was a pugnacious man, small but strong. He leaned across the table and punched McAlister in the face.

McAlister: 'You hit me when my hands were down.'

Hill (putting his hands behind his back): 'My hands are down now.'

McAlister rushed around the table and grappled with Hill. McAlister was six feet tall, Hill was eight years younger and more powerful. Locked together, they swayed around the room, crashing against the table and wall. Blood stained their clothes and splashed on Iredale and Smith.

Hill was intent upon chucking McAlister out into Martin Place but Smith hauled on Hill's coat-tails. Ten minutes' fighting ended with McAlister sprawled on his back on the floor and Hill standing over him, unmarked. He then left the room.

When McAlister arose he called out, 'Coward!' and made to follow Hill, but Smith and Iredale stood against the locked door. Hill resigned his selector's job on the spot, Mayne replacing him. As was said, Mayne's first act was to put himself into the 1912 side for England. He played in one Test and never batted. He never played in a Test against England in Australia and was exceedingly lucky to have gone to England in 1921.

McAlister embarked from the Melbourne express at Flinders Street next morning with the greatest black eye ever seen outside a boxing ring. Hill was given three cheers by the Melbourne crowd when next he appeared on that ground. A fortnight later the Sydney crowd repeated the greeting when he played his last Test on that ground, making 20 and then eight, clean bowled by Foster on a 'sticky'.

Throughout the row with the Big Six there was no doubt where the sympathy of the crowd lay. As I said, feeling between players and legislators had been building up for years, and continued well into my playing time; but things are different now. A younger group of Board men – and Bradman would have played a prominent part in this when chairman – are much closer to the players and give them generous treatment. In a recent meeting of the Board, in 1976 in Brisbane, Australian captain Greg Chappell sat in on the Board meeting – something that his brother, Ian, when skipper, had long recommended.

One outcome of the dispute was that it put an end to Trumper's playing big cricket in Australia. The war came, of course, and he went with Arthur Sims's team to New Zealand; but he bowed out of official Australian cricket as he would have liked – with his cobbers Hill, Armstrong, Carter, Cotter and Ransford, and in the best tradition of Australian life – mateship.

This chapter gives me the chance to comment on the crisis that Kerry Packer brought into international cricket, and cricket at every level, with his move in 1977 to disembowel Test cricket, which is what his action really means. It provides the chance, also, to compare the Packer crisis with that of 1912 and the Big Six.

I have long known the Packer family. Robert Clive, the grandfather of Kerry, began the *Guardian* (since defunct) with Sir Joynton Smith, a cockney who came to Australia and made his fortune, and Claude Mackay, later a very close friend of mine and a wonderful spinner of yarns, in Sydney in the 'twenties. An associated newspaper was *Smith's Weekly*. Joynton was a tough customer. Claude told me the story of how he used to delight in asking people when he met them to pick his glass eye. One chap did one day and Joynton was amazed and asked the chap how he had done it. 'Well,' he said, 'I noticed the look of human kindness in the glass one.'

I had my first newspaper job on the *Guardian* and loved it. It looked like coming to an abrupt end one day when I dropped a paste-pot on the concrete floor outside Robert Clive's office. It went off like a miniature atom-bomb and a visibly shaken Mr Packer emerged to know who had done it. 'Please, sir,' I said, 'I did.' 'Go in and tell Mr Molesworth to sack you straight away,' said Mr Packer. Vol Molesworth was our editor, a slick newspaperman, and he didn't beat around the bush.

'Go upstairs and get your money,' said the snappy Vol and, laden with holiday pay, several weeks in lieu of notice and other things, I went sadly home and spent the next few weeks, disconsolate, on Bondi Beach. Then came a telephone call. 'Is that you, Fingleton?' it said. I admitted identity, whereupon the voice said, 'It's Vol Molesworth here. Where have you been lately?' 'Please, sir,' I said, 'you sacked me.' 'Don't be a fool,' said the editor, 'no one takes any notice of the bloody sack in the *Guardian*. You come in at once.'

So I went in, thankfully, but took good care to keep out of Mr Packer's way, just in case. Kerry's father, Sir Frank, and I served our cadetship together on the *Guardian*. Kerry's brother, Clyde, I knew as an agreeable young man in the Parliamentary Press Gallery at Canberra. He has since gone to live in the United States. I played golf with Kerry at Canberra, and at Harrogate one day, as I umpired, I gave him a caught behind decision, thus revoking the stumping which he also got. He said he would sooner have had the stumping, as it would have looked much better in the Press!

I don't think his father, Sir Frank, would have thought much of Kerry's attempt to monopolize the cricket world for television. Frank would have pondered on the economics of the venture. When they asked Clyde about it in the other hemisphere he said brightly, 'I am not my brother's keeper.'

One principle in the Big Six's row with officialdom, in Trumper's time, was based on how the players resented officials, who had been non-players, getting the rich food while they had to be content with the crumbs. Joe Darling told how the officials and their guests used to hog the food and drink at Test matches while the players, due to go out on the field again within an allotted time, could not get a cup of afternoon tea. Joe, too, didn't think much of the many officials who limelighted themselves by inviting a covey of business friends along to the matches and invaded the players' accommodation.

The principles of those times were vastly different to the one principle – money – that actuated Kerry Packer and the cricketers who threw in their lot with him. Kerry wanted to get a monopoly of cricket on television in Australia, which would have given him a monopoly on sport, as he already has the Australian Open golf and Wimbledon and other tennis. The players were lured by the prospect of picking up seemingly easy money and this, for many of them, towards the end of their playing days.

I have mixed with the Packer camp in recent times and, obviously, have been 'duchessed', a term Australians use when they go to England on a business or political trip and the expectant English turn on the lavish treatment for them. But if I was, so were all the other Pressmen, the police and the myriads of televisions crews. Kerry, obviously, has a limitless pit of dollars to spend, and it is anybody's guess how much this first season of his has cost him in Australia.

For all his outward cheeriness he must be worried about the venture. His crowds have not been big in Australia and for all the claims of revolutionizing cricket on television (I had many chances of observing this while in hospital on my return from England in 1977), I don't think he has. He has a multiplicity of cameras on the job, his commentators – Benaud, Trueman, Cosier, Lawry and Stackpole – are understandably very agreeable and laudatory about it all on the air, but the only thing extra I noticed was a cameraman and an interviewer who invited the outcoming batsman to 'tell all' about his dismissal. I am still waiting for the batsman and, for that matter, the Pressman who says, 'It was a simple straight ball and I missed it.' The ball always seems to cut or swing or do something phenomenal.

I liked what I saw of Packer's cricket but there was something missing. Tony Greig, a very fair man, volunteered to me what a wonderful series that between Australia and India was. And that is what Packer's cricket must always lack. It is not Test cricket. But Packer is not a man to give up, nor will he go away. His very name is anathema to cricket officials. His party was officially offered 200 free tickets to see the fourth Test between India and Australia in Sydney, but in the Brewongle stand, which at that moment didn't exist. It was demolished. For all that, many Packer men did see the Test.

Kerry Packer is so far committed in money that he will go on, but I think his future is in one-day matches and those at night. He told me he is thinking of having his players wear coloured flannels for night matches. He is full of ideas and is of that generation of young men with assets who think the old order is only there to be changed. He has intense loyalty from his players, whom he has treated most generously.

Another difficulty seems to be creeping in. Will the players of all countries, as happened with England in Pakistan recently, refuse to play against Packer men? I don't think even a judge of the English High Court can order international selectors to choose certain men. At the moment of writing, an Australian team has just been chosen to tour the West Indies – who will play all Packer men. Our Board has erred in this. I advocated that we should seek a postponement of the tour for a few years but while our Board men righteously said to me it was purely a concern for the West Indies who played for them, I reasoned on other grounds. I know the intensity of Tests there, and we are building up a team of young men at present who could well be shattered by the pace they will meet there. Our bowlers will get similar treatment.

The West Indies are undoubtedly the world's best team at the moment. They came to Australia to get every dollar they could out of the Packer matches and with the exception of one reverse in Adelaide they look like doing it. They are intent on building up real estate back in their homeland and have imposed a 10.30 p.m. curfew on themselves which they religiously observe. They have an inspiring skipper in Clive

Lloyd (I noticed that Greig never set a field for a West Indian bowler unless he conferred first with Lloyd). There is edge in the games, as there always will be when money is the only consideration, but far too much wide bowling by the Australians. I think Mr Packer, who has a genius of a groundsman in Mr Maley, must consider limiting the width of his pitch, as they do in England in one-day games, so that a bowler must attack the stumps. Tony Greig got very fed up in Sydney at the wide Australian bowling.

It is an interesting facet of the case that all players of my generation abhor the Packer cricket. I don't think this is 'sour grapes'. They know that cricket must be served at every level and that this costs money which stems from Test cricket, in the main. Then again, modern Test players do very well as it is out of cricket. There are many avenues to be exploited and Trumper's generation would be amazed at the sums paid now to play Test cricket. Modern Test cricketers have nothing to grumble about as they get the best of everything and every consideration. Greg Chappell, as captain, was sitting in on Board meetings after the players had decided to defect.

The news of the pending happening was the best-kept secret in sport. The secret first leaked out in South Africa in April 1977, just as the Australian players in the plot were beginning their tour of England. Those Australians were well thrashed by a better team, in all ways, but they must have been ill-suited, mentally, to play for their country. The hotels in England were a mass of intrigue and rumours, with legal men, Packer men and players being summoned to telephones, and Pressmen all mingling and conjecturing. Thomson, when he came to bat at Trent Bridge, got a tremendous ovation on the morning it had been announced that he had withdrawn from his Packer contract. It was obvious where the sympathy of the cricket public lay. Kerry was roundly hooted that day he appeared at Harrogate, in 'Boycott' country.

It could turn out that the Packer imbroglio will cleanse the game and house of cricket. The players were indulging in too many gimmicks, too much 'sledging' and too much bad language for the liking of those who think cricket should be superior to all this. And one could also include that ignoble form of slobbering adulation that inevitably follows whenever a player takes a catch or a wicket. I would hate to think of how Bill O'Reilly would have reacted had his fellows tried to slobber over him whenever he got a batsman out.

Kerry Packer would not tell me where he would get his new players to replace his many injuries and retirements which would come in due course. 'Don't worry,' he said, 'I will get them.' Cricket officials have tried to secure their players by new bonds. Perhaps Kerry has read Aldous Huxley's *Brave New World* and believed in the Bokanovskified Process and will develop buds from his champions – and he has many of those, including the two Richards. But I foresee a lonely old cricket age ahead of them all. Whereas players of the Trumper era and my own knew and know the marvellous feelings of 'mateship', the Packer players will miss all this, and will be generally shunned by established cricket. I wonder if they will then think that the money was worth it all. I doubt it.

12

Trumper's Benefit

When Trumper had his benefit match on the Sydney Cricket Ground in early February 1913 it was noted that the sporting public of Australia rose splendidly to acknowledge the great services of Trumper to Australian cricket.

The game began on a Friday, and though intermittent rain fell on Saturday and affected the gate it nevertheless drew some £890 from 13,000 spectators. From the other States, too, contributions came most generously, until a handsome total for those days was reached.

Trumper, it was said, had experienced many thrilling moments during his long and eventful career, but the Saturday's reception of him where he had played so many of his unforgettable innings capped them all. He led the NSW side, which included Macartney, Noble (who had come out of retirement for the occasion), Hordern, Bardsley, Collins, Carter and Barbour. The Rest side was led by Clem Hill and included J. N. Crawford, a great all-rounder, Armstrong, Whitty, Johnnie Moyes (later to become a famous Australian cricket historian and well-known broadcaster), Vernon Ransford and Jack Ryder.

When Trumper emerged from the pavilion the crowd rose to him and gave him a vociferous welcome which lasted for some minutes. The band played 'For He's a Jolly Good Fellow' and the Rest of Australia team, with Clem Hill leading them, gave him three cheers. There was another outburst from the crowd, which dwindled away as Trumper took block, after bowing again to the crowd in his acknowledgement of the greatest compliment that had ever been paid him.

Naturally, Trumper was overcome by his great welcome. I asked Jack Ryder to tell me about it, and he claims that he had Victor out LBW for a duck but didn't appeal. 'What, Jack,' I said, 'you didn't appeal and you a Victorian, too?' Jack overlooked that and told me that when Trumper got to the other end he said, 'Thanks, Jack.' One other story I heard was that somebody did appeal for LBW against Trumper and the whole fielding side shouted out, 'Not out!' Whatever happened, Trumper got a century and was not out in the second innings, a fitting farewell to a famous ground by, perhaps, its most famous son. Jack Ryder got eight wickets in a drawn game. Batting brilliantly, Charlie Macartney got 91 and Eric Barbour made 86. Macartney and Barbour put on 138 for the second wicket for NSW. The camera caught Trumper and Macartney going out to field and those who know the ground today will wonder at the pair going up steps out of the Members' Pavilion to get on to the ground. The reason was that a bicycle track ran around the ground but when it went there was no further need for the steps and so they went, too.

I have a book in my possession which is a valuable journal of the contributors to the Trumper fund. There is a lot of childish scribbling on blank pages but it tells the history of the Victor Trumper Testimonial Fund with Henry Moses, junior, as honorary treasurer, and the first contribution is on 20 December 1912. I was interested to notice that the ninth donor to the fund was Mr Justice Street, grandfather-in-law of mine and later Chief Justice of NSW. His son Ken was also Chief Justice, as is now Sir Laurence Street, my brother-in-law. Sir Phillip Street gave his two guineas to the fund on 23 December and the list includes many of the famous family names of Sydney and the country of that period. It amounted to £1106 19s. 3d. on 5 May 1913. That was purely from subscriptions. To it were added the receipts from the match and from other State associations. Plum Warner sent a cheque from England, the great Dally Messenger, the footballer, also contributed, as did innumerable schools, staffs and junior cricket clubs. I was interested to see in the list Ern Williams, who never tired of talking to us at Waverley about Trumper and who paid many subscriptions for junior players, including my own, into the Waverley club at a time of what we can euphemistically call a credit squeeze. Ern was a hard but good judge and none but the deserving got out of his classifications of 'grubbers' and 'shysters'.

Wolfes Schnappes was then a keen sponsor in cricket, and indeed continued their sponsorship well into my time, and that firm duplicated the awards the players had gained in that match. Collins, Moyes and Barbour each contributed to the fund what they had won. The players on both sides went on the Hill and sold autographed photos and postcards of Trumper. The NSW bookstall sold 2065 of these at 2/- per dozen and 245 sketch cards at 8d. per dozen. There was a lovely old chap who manufactured glazed photographs of Trumper for the occasion and they were autographed by all the teams. He was keen on cricket and to this day one of my most prized possessions is one of these which he gave me one day at the SCG. I like the two entries, 'A Newcastle schoolboy: 2/6; One of Trumper's Pupils: 1/-.'

A sequel to this subscription list was a court case, before Mr Justice Pring and a jury, in which Thomas John Houghton claimed £111 7s. from Trumper for commission alleged to be due to him as agent and working secretary for the defendant. Houghton appeared to conduct his own case; Trumper, who pleaded never indebted, was represented by Mr James, instructed by Messrs H. J. R. Clayton.

The plaintiff in his opening said that the sum was for commission at the rate of 10 per cent on the sum of £1113 13s. 2d. collected by a citizens' committee, formed by plaintiff at the request, it was alleged, of the defendant, and for work done for the defendant in connection with the Trumper testimonial fund. He claimed only on £1113 13s. 2d., the amount collected by the committee and not on the net sum received by the defendant, Trumper, £2980. He claimed he had worked five solid months for the defendant and had not yet received the price of a postage stamp for his services. (Oddly, the journal I have, composed by Mr Moses, shows on the expenditure side the sum of £10 8s. 4d. paid to a T. J. Houghton on 24 December 1912 for 'Postages'. I wonder where this journal was during the case, as it might have been a valuable piece of evidence.)

Houghton said he earned his living as an organizer, advertising agent and journalist. Early in December 1912 he met Mr Hanson Carter at his place of business in Oxford Street Bondi Junction, and later saw Mr Trumper, who said his match would be a failure if it were left to the NSW Cricket Association to organize. He alleged that Trumper also told him that Mr Bowden, the secretary of the association, would do his best to make it a failure. The defendant then said: 'You are just the man I want to run it for me. You form a committee and I'll give you ten per cent of all I get. If it is left to the association I won't get as much as Charlie Turner got.'

Witness said: 'All right; I'll do my best.' In order to get to work right away he asked the defendant for names of gentlemen who might assist him in forming a committee. Defendant wrote the names of a number of gentlemen on the back of an envelope. Witness interviewed these gentlemen, and issued a circular convening a meeting of Victor Trumper's friends and admirers to be held on 16 December 1912.

His Honour, Mr Justice Pring: Have you got that circular?

Houghton: No, it can't be found.

How valuable the book I have might have been in evidence then! But the journal wasn't there, and Houghton's case seemed to slip with the judge and the jury when he could not produce the circular which he claimed convened the meeting. The circular, he said, bore the signatures of H. H. Massie and T. W. Garrett as conveners, for which he had their consent. The meeting took place at the Hotel Australia and those present formed themselves into a committee for the purpose of assisting in the movement. An executive was appointed, with Mr T. W. Garrett as Hon. Secretary. Garrett had previously told the meeting that he would only accept office on condition that Houghton was appointed working secretary and did all the work. Mr Garrett proposed that and Houghton was elected.

The committee held numerous meetings. Houghton issued 1627 subscription lists and 300 quarto circulars, to as many persons; he kept the books (that doesn't seem to fit in with this journal), did all the correspondence and other work. During Christmas week 1912 and New Year week 1913 the whole of his time was occupied with this work. He called at the offices of the SCG every day and also at the office of Messrs Barry and Morris, solicitors. Sometimes as many as 60 or 70 names appeared on the subscription lists, which were inserted in the newspapers. When the fund was about to be closed, at the end of April, he asked Trumper: 'What about the money?' and Trumper, he said, replied to him: 'Don't you worry; you'll be paid all right.'

This went on for some considerable time. Later on Trumper told him it would take a long time to fix up the Trust and the investment, but he might write to the committee for something to keep him going. He wrote to the committee and received a reply, in which it was stated that the committee regretted that it could not use the fund in any way except for the benefit of Trumper and also placed on record its high appreciation of the services he had rendered and expressed regret that it did not have the power to pay him anything. The judge, in his summing up, agreed with Trumper that he was never indebted, the jury thought likewise, and that was that.

In a leading article, the Sydney *Telegraph* said:

The refusal of the court on Tuesday to uphold a claim for 10 per cent commission by the organizer of the Trumper testimonial is a satisfactory intimation that the promotion of such schemes is not to be recognized as an ordinary business. Whatever gratitude, not to speak of fairness, might prompt the recipient of such a compliment to do by way of rewarding him who procures it for him is another question. If it could be proved that a clear agreement existed under which the promoter of a testimonial was to have a share of the proceeds, large or small, that of course would have to be honoured like any other legitimate contract. But what this case shows is that commission is not chargeable in the ordinary way, as it would be in the sale of a property. Even where there is a contract the terms should in common fairness be made known so that the public may know exactly what they are subscribing their money for. Were commission chargeable without any contract, however, the promotion of testimonials would become a regular profession and the burden of civilized existence increased by the addition of another needless trouble. We would have cute men erecting pedestals upon which to put all sorts of person just for the money to be made by themselves out of the work . . . It is the system that demands condemnation, not the particular application of it to the Trumper case or any other case.

So Mr Houghton got 'nowt' and the Trumper Trust was not disposed to be generous in any way than for the purpose of the fund. I have told the tale of how Trumper sent an old work-mate to the Trust with a note saying that he had strung bats for him, and was now on hard times, but he fared no better than anybody else.

The Trust was set up in 1913 and dissolved in April 1966. The sum of £2950 13s. 3d. was placed in the hands of Trustees appointed by NSW Cricket Association to hold and invest, the income to be paid to Victor Trumper during his lifetime and, after his death, to his wife, Sarah Ann Trumper, and after her death to the children of the marriage. The last surviving member of the family was Victor Trumper Jnr, and an amount of £1268 9s. 4d. was transferred to him. From the fund, a sum of 12 guineas a month was paid to Victor's widow until her death a few years prior to 1966.

13

The Last Great Innings

Trumper's last great innings was played in Christchurch, New Zealand, in February and March 1914, when he hit 293 in what was declared to be the outstanding innings ever played in New Zealand. He died almost within the year at the age of 37.

One would think Herbie Collins would be an acceptable authority on that innings, for he was in the team, but I read an article by him once that must be dubious, to say the least. He said that Trumper took a bat offered him by a schoolboy as he was going out to bat and made his 293 with that – and towards the end of his innings with only half of it, as the bat broke badly. I doubt this very much as, thanks to Walter Hadlee, who sought them out, I handled two bats of Trumper's in Christchurch and one of them, which had a bad split up one side of it but had been repaired, I believe to be the one that Trumper used in his 293 innings – at least up to when he had reached 130, when it split and Trumper changed it.

Another bat I saw was that used by Trumper in his preceding tour of New Zealand in 1904–5 season. It is now in the possession of Mr J. C. Saunders and, apart from bearing all the scores Trumper made in New Zealand on that tour, it carries all the autographs of the Australian team with the inscription, 'From J. J. Kelly to F. C. Raphael in remembrance of Victor Trumper. 11/3/05.' Mr F. C. Raphael was secretary of the New Zealand Cricket Council from 1901 to 1914.

The first bat, in which I was more interested, belongs to Mr O. A. Y. Johnston, a prominent Christchurch businessman and a leading golfer and golf administrator. It was given to him on the Sunday of the Canterbury match, the day after

Trumper made his 293 – which included three sixes and 44 fours.

Mr Johnston's father, I was told, was one of several Christ-church men asked to provide car transport for a visit by the Australians to *Otohuna*, the home of Sir Heaton Rhodes. The party later went on to *Kinloch*, the Little River home of the Buchan family, to see Martian, the outstanding sire of the time. When the party returned to Christchurch O. A. Y. Johnston, then aged 13, was asked by Trumper – with whom he had kept company on the trip – if he would like a bat because, Trumper said, he seemed to be keen on cricket. Trumper gave him the bat he had used and damaged the previous day, with advice on how to have it repaired. The bat was duly repaired and its proud new owner batted with it on several occasions later, when a member of the first eleven at Christ's College. I think this story a more likely one than the one written by Collins, who does not appear to be a very reliable reporter. In the same story he says that Trumper began his innings by hitting the first ball from Bennett for six. Not so. The news-papers of that time used to give a batsman's name and follow with all his scoring strokes opposite his name, followed by the manner of his dismissal, and his total. This shows that Trumper started his big innings with a single.

The tour of New Zealand was due to the enterprise of Sir Arthur Sims, an old Canterbury boy, and in his day one of the best batsmen Canterbury turned out. For some years his wool business necessitated extensive travelling between New Zealand, Australia and England, and his love of and enthusiasm for cricket enabled him to bring over to New Zealand the flower of Australian cricket. Trumper, Armstrong (who held the record score made in New Zealand of 335 for the Melbourne club against Southland in 1906), Ransford, Noble and young players such as Mailey, Waddy, Dr Dolling (later to be an Australian selector), the famous all-rounder J. N. Crawford, Les Cody and Bert Collins, with Sims himself, made up the Australian team. Reese captained the local side and the New Zealand *Referee* of the time enthused over the play :

Those who went to Lancaster Park on Saturday got the

cricket feast of a lifetime. There were probably few in the big crowd who had ever seen anything like it, and doubtless the great majority will never see its equal again. There is only one Trumper in the world, and after watching him – for over three hours – execute his magic-like strokes all round the wicket one could subscribe enthusiastically to the sentiment conveyed in his being styled 'The incomparable Victor'. Talk about the champagne of cricket! It was all that, with an electric sparkle running through it all the way. One might enthuse over it to the extent of columns and yet not be guilty of exaggeration.

It was a bit chilly towards the close, but neither the batsmen nor the fieldsmen noticed it. They were too busy. The wicket was in first-class order, Armstrong said, and he was in long enough to know. At any rate, Trumper liked it, and Sims had no fault to find with it, and he was there long enough for his acquaintance to ripen into intimacy. The outfield was accused on Friday of being on the slow side, but Trumper demonstrated on Saturday that this was only a rumour, for the lively manner in which the ball bumped and cleared the picket fence might almost have suggested that it was hard.

There was a big crowd to watch the play, probably nearly 5000, for the takings were £248. This assembly would include some two or three thousand who only get to cricket matches on great occasions, and they got their money's worth.

To return to the play. Canterbury had done well on the first day to get five of the opposition out for 105, but the champion batsmen were yet to come, and probably no one imagined that with Sims and Cody in, and with top-notchers like Trumper, Armstrong, Ransford and Crawford to come, this success would be maintained. And so it was quickly demonstrated – for though Cody did not stay long the next partnership between Armstrong and Sims put on nearly 100, and was the forerunner of what was to follow – a partnership that produced 433 runs in a little over three hours, and a display of batting that was an absolute revelation even to

L

many who had seen the world's greatest batsmen.

The cricket scribe's vocabulary is quite inadequate to describe Trumper's innings. Much of the daring that electrified the cricket world a decade or more ago had departed. He is said to have mellowed with age, and strengthened his defence. It may be suggested that the mellowing process has left absolutely untarnished the superlativeness of his strokes. His defence may be sounder. One can easily believe it but that 'age has withered or custom staled' his remarkable powers as a batsman is unbelievable after Saturday's display. His driving? It was equal to that of great batsmen who have specialized in the stroke. More often than not the only description of its power would be the pace at which the ball would be seen travelling to the fence and the remarkably short space of time it took to get there.

His late cutting was a marvel. Bennett's perfect-length ball just outside the off stump – the most deadly ball in his repertoire – was flicked away anywhere between slip and point with the ease and precision of timing that was absolutely artistic. But probably the most astonishing feature of his batting was his play on the on-side. Balls just clear of the leg-stump, whether they kept low or bounced high, were unerringly despatched towards the on-fence, and the manner in which he kept the high-bouncing balls all along the sward and yet got the same power into the stroke seemed nothing short of jugglery. Only cricketers could appreciate the difficulty of it. Altogether, it was a display of batting which for sound defence and purity of stroke with the maximum aggressiveness and minimum of risk has never been equalled in Christchurch.

The cricket gods, then, must have smiled on Trumper that day – and rightly so, for it was to be his last big innings of such a nature, although he was later to play another double-century innings at Invercargill. Bill Ferguson was the scorer at Christchurch and gave his scoring graph of Trumper's boundary strokes to the local newspaper. I reproduce it here, and it is to be noted that Trumper hit a six directly over point. Also

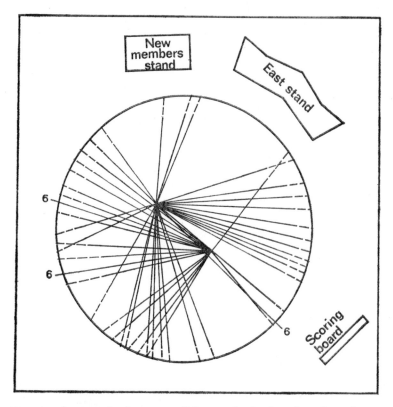

Diagram showing the direction of Trumper's chief strokes (forty-four fours and three sixes) in his huge score of 293, compiled in three hours and ten minutes, against Canterbury in New Zealand in 1914.

noticeable is that from the score-board end he didn't hit a single boundary on the off or cover drive from that end, but the flow of on-side boundaries is truly staggering. I have seen a Test played at Christchurch between England and New Zealand and I have never before heard such chirruping as the spectators indulged themselves in in the grandstand during the game. They had something to chirp about that 1914 day.

I had mixed thoughts as I held the two Trumper bats in Christchurch. The one in my left hand in the photo reproduced on the back flap of the present book is the bat used by Trumper

in part of his 293 innings and which was subsequently given to
the small lad, Johnston, whose father had it repaired. The
borers have got into it and it is now badly marked by them.
The other bat is in fairly good condition, considering its age.

I was most struck – apart from the thrill of just holding
them – by their weight. They are much heavier than batsmen
in my time would use, although moderns now go in for
weighty bats. The handles are thick, unrubbered, and one could
not imagine a prominent batsman, particularly a classical one,
choosing such unpretentious bats. The point that impressed
me about them was that Trumper must have had wrists of
steel to wield them so dexterously and execute such delicate
shots.

14
Death of a Cricketer

Trumper suffered an attack of scarlet fever when he was 30 and this may have had some connection with the illness from which he died – Bright's disease – at the age of 37. His wife wrote to some English friends, the Glossops of Sheffield, some months after his death :

About October 1914 cricket had just commenced. He had played all Saturday afternoon and on Sunday I noticed his ankles were a little swollen. It worried me at the time and I threatened to bring in the doctor. He begged me not to worry, he was all right, but after great persuasion he promised to go to a doctor himself, an old school-mate. I was anxious all day for him to come home, as he was usually bright and happy when coming home. He said, 'Nothing serious wrong with me. Probably a cold on the kidneys,' and he would have to diet himself for a while. He knew I had an awful dread of Bright's Disease. Of course, all his worry about business did not help him and unfortunately he had tons of worry since he first commenced business. At times he seemed tired, very tired, but looked well and I thought it was worry all the time. Vic trusted everybody. He was too honest for business and trusted everybody to the last degree . . .

He said he never would go into business again and I thought that was the end of his worry. In March 1915 we went to Collaroy Beach, not far from here, for a fortnight. I thought it would do the children and my poor Vic good, but were there only two days and he did not seem at all well, the sea-air being too strong for him. At once we came home

and I made Vic seek the advice of a specialist, who ordered
him to bed. That was the beginning of March, and he was
in bed for three months and got along beautifully. He was
always naturally cheerful and was in great spirits when all
the swelling disappeared.

He was very tired of bed and insisted on the doctor allowing him to get up. The doctor was afraid, it was the beginning of June, rather cold, and he was afraid of a chill.
Evidently he did get the chill somehow, and swelling commenced to appear again. The doctor ordered him into
hospital (which I think was a mistake) for treatment with
'steam', which could not be done at home, on 21 June. The
doctor thought he was going to pull through but my poor
Vic on Sunday night, 27 June, about 10.30 p.m. to their great
surprise in the hospital, took a nasty turn, became un-
conscious, and remained so until he died at 10 a.m. on
Monday, 28 June.

On the Sunday about 6 p.m. Vic and I were talking about
you all and making arrangements to leave for England this
March and what a great surprise we thought it would be to
you all. We intended not to let you know until we arrived
in England. As soon as his friends knew he was in hospital
(he had been there one week), they arranged a meeting and
decided to send Vic and his family to England. They thought
that this trip would prolong his life for a number of years,
although they expected he would never play cricket again.
He started sport too young. They had sent him word of the
promised trip that morning and he was delighted telling me
all about it. We looked forward to another trip, he had
always promised me that. He loved England. That same afternoon, his last afternoon, he told me he had such a lot to do
for me and the children and he would not rest content until
he saw his boy an 'Oxford University Boy'. How he loved
that baby nobody knows and to lose that 'Daddy' at 18
months old! What a father to lose and what have the
children lost! Nancy was always 'Mummy's girl' but baby
loved Vic and always wanted his Daddy. You would love
baby Vic, he is so affectionate. Surely after eight years God

sent him as a consolation for what was coming. We hope he will be spared to me. His grandparents say he is the picture of his daddy when a baby. A thorough boy and full of sport already. I really don't think there could be another Vic although you could not imagine a son of Vic being anything but good. Anyway, I shall try and do my very best for them.

Poor Nancy, of course she can always remember him. Rather quiet in her way, not much to say, but a great comfort to her mother now. I know she frets a great deal about her Daddy at times. He was never known to have been cross with her.

From yours affectionately, Annie Trumper.

It is an odd thing that so little has been named after Trumper. John Hook, of Paddington, gave me some interesting information on this. Due to his correspondence with the developers, they named three of the units they built in the Trumper Park development 'Ransford', 'Bardsley' and 'Cotter' – all of whom were Trumper's contemporaries. The grandstand at Chatswood Oval, where Trumper finished his club cricket with a string of single centuries, was named Trumper Stand. Nothing at the Sydney Cricket Ground, which saw so many of his brilliant innings, was named after him. The secretary of the SCG, Mr John Wood, gave me much useful information about the ground but said nothing was named after Trumper. The only reminder of him is something out of view, behind the Sheridan Stand. Sheridan was a trustee and later Managing Trustee until 1910, when he died. People on the Hill contributed to a grey marble plaque with gold lettering: 'In Memory of Victor Trumper died at Sydney 28th June, 1915, aged 38 years. Erected by his friends and admirers.' It was fixed to the back of the Sheridan Stand and is seen by few. I have never seen it and I know the SCG very well. Until Mr Wood told me of it, I never knew it existed. Trumper's age, incidentally, they got one year wrong.

At Sydney there are the Bradman and Noble stands. There are also plaques on the Sydney ground to the memory of Noble,

Kippax and McCabe, all trustees of the ground; but nothing visible to perpetuate the memory of Trumper. I have in mind the Brewongle Stand; but Mr Wood can't tell me how it came by that name. I sought the help of the Institute of Aboriginal Affairs in Canberra and their job wasn't helped by the fact that there are over 500 different dialects in the aboriginal language. Mr Keith Sinclair, of the Institute, tracked it down finally and came up with the information that it means 'Camping Ground'. Alan Davidson put it into the news once when he hit a ball from M. C. Cowdrey up near the flag-pole of the stand, one of the biggest hits I have seen. It would be a just gesture to an immortal of the game if that Trumper plaque were brought from the rear of the Sheridan Stand, once named the Smokers' Stand, put in front of the Brewongle Stand, where it could be seen, and the stand re-named the Trumper Stand, late the Brewongle Stand, on a plaque added to the Trumper one. That would perpetuate both Trumper and the aboriginals.

I walked through the Long Room at Lord's one day in 1975 looking for relics of Trumper. There were bats used by Hirst, Rhodes, Hayward, Miss Mary Willett, Hobbs, Woolley, Grace and Hendren, a blue (why not pink?) ball used by women at the turn of the century, and, sure enough, the last bat used by Trumper in England in 1909. The maker was F. H. Ayres. Trumper had given the bat to Walter Brearley who gave it to Lord's.

There are portraits of Sammy Woods, Sir Donald Bradman (painted by R. Hannaford and presented to Lord's by the Commercial Bank of Australia in 1973), William Beldham, Alfred Mynn, John Wisden, a huge one of I. D. Walker, and, naturally, Thomas Lord, who saved Lord's from the developers, who have swept over London. But there is no painting of Trumper, although there is a photograph that seems to have been the work of a capable photographer, the picture of Trumper jumping out to drive. It should inspire some artist to paint it and present it to Lord's.

There is a cabinet in the Lord's Memorial, the museum just across the way from the Pavilion, which gives Trumper's figures; but there is a mistake there: it says Trumper averaged

94 in five innings in South Africa in five Tests in 1910–11. It was in Australia. In the case in memory of Repton cricketers is a cap worn by H. S. Love in 1932 and a pair of skimpy pads. 'Pads like these were worn by Victor Trumper', reads the caption. There is an Australian blazer worn in 1909 and a cap and blazer worn by Trumper and given to Lord's by Mrs Trumper. 'But figures,' runs a note on him, 'fail to give a true idea of his greatness. With the exception of Sir Donald Bradman, he is acknowledged as the most brilliant of all Australian batsmen, able to score under all conditions of weather and pitch. On a sticky wicket, he was almost more to be feared than on one in good condition and he was never afraid to resort to unorthodox methods when orthodoxy failed. He remains a legendary figure in Australia, one whose game rests not only on his greatness as a batsman but also on his qualities as a man.'

Alongside the Repton cabinet is a painting of Charles Dickens at Gadshill Place, near Rochester, where he lived from 1856 to 1870, and he is seen here bowling the first ball in a match in a meadow behind his house. It was his habit to award a guinea for a boundary hit. His son, Sir Henry Dickens, wrote: 'My father used to take the part of scorer in the games played here and he was sustained in his arduous job by the "cooling drinks" provided by the guests who were staying in the house at the time or by neighbours who came to watch the game.' Charles could not have been bowling for a catch. All the fieldsmen have their caps raised on high in salute as Charles sent down the first ball – underarm.

I was interested also in the memorial to Harry Altham, who 'served the game with distinction as an administrator, player and coach and concerned himself especially with young cricketers, for whom a bursary has been endowed which bears his name'. Typical of Harry, who never tired of quoting Latin tags, it ends '*Humanitis Sedulatis Auctoritas*'. Rain at Lord's means far from a dull day. But I would love to hear that a painted picture of Trumper driving is to be hung there.

The cricket world was stunned at news of Trumper's death,

which came in the private hospital of St Vincent's, Darling-hurst, near Paddington. Tributes, even during the war when pages of the daily newspapers were filled with columns and photographs of people killed, came from all over the world.

His funeral was huge. I must mention Reg Fusedale, who also went to Crown Street School, and who, with a number of later sporting celebrities, used to steal into the Sydney Cricket Ground through the adjacent Show Ground, and saw all Trumper's big innings there. They all idolized Trumper, and Reg's biggest sporting thrill was to get a century not out for Sydney against Gordon at Chatswood one Saturday afternoon in 1909. Next Saturday Trumper got 130 and Reg was thrilled when he went into Trumper's ill-fated sports-goods store, then in Hunter Street, to be personally greeted by Trumper.

Reg Fusedale reminds me also of another great character on the Sydney Hill, Johnny O'Hara, of Paddington. He rivalled 'Yabba' in his popularity and, the possessor of a stentorian voice, he would greet anything outstanding with the cry of a peacock. He was a great bird mimic but best of all on the peacock with his 'Keogh, keogh' which would echo across the ground and was so good an imitation that the peacocks in the Sydney Zoo, just across from the SCG, and then situated where the Sydney High School now is, would answer him back. Johnny would go to work whenever Trumper hit a spate of boundaries. Unlike 'Yabba', he was never crude.

Reg, a great character, is pushing into the late eighties very vigorously, with a daily swim and a good round of golf. He maintains that in Trumper's famous 'dog shot' the batsman lifted his back foot to clamp down on yorkers. Another who went to Crown Street was 'Snowy' Baker, possibly Australia's best all-round sportsman, who was beaten in the final of a middleweight boxing championship in an Olympic Games by the Essex captain, J. W. H. T. Douglas.

Horse-drawn vehicles were the thing in Sydney in 1915 and Reg was a commercial traveller. In his sulky he waited at Fort Macquarie for the funeral to come across the Harbour. He said the funeral cortège stretched for three-and-a-half miles. Many mourners marched to Regent Street, Paddington, took the tram to Charing Cross, formed up again, and marched ahead to Waverley Cemetery.

It was the biggest funeral ever known at Waverley. Every cricketer of any note in NSW seemed to be there. The chief mourners were Victor's father, Charles, and brothers Syd and Charlie. Hanson Carter was the funeral director and the pall-bearers were F. A. Iredale, J. A. O'Connor, M. A. Noble, Warren Bardsley, Dr H. V. Hordern, A. Cotter, C. T. B. Turner, C. G. Macartney, C. Kelleway and S. E. Gregory. Giving the long list of cricketers present, plus sportsmen of other codes, Jack Davis wrote: 'This may be interpreted not merely as an expression of the admiration they felt for him as a cricketer but as a token of the affection he inspired among all classes of men who knew him. Mere words cannot tell those who come into sport in Australia's future the feelings which Victor Trumper's personal charm and batsmanship inspired in the hearts of men and boys of his time.'

The Rev. E. H. Cranswick, of St Paul's Church of England, Chatswood, who read the burial service, subsequently delivered at the grave a singularly appropriate eulogy of the departed hero. He exalted him as son, husband and father. He described him as the hero of all assembled to pay the last honour to his memory, and to thousands of others. Victor, he said, possessed many noble qualities, and these made him the great sportsman he had been all through his career. He played the game as it should be played, and though he would be remembered for many things, nothing could be greater than his wonderful spirit of sportsmanship.

And so he was laid to rest in the tranquil cemetery of Waverley, perched high on the Bronte cliffs and looking out to sea across the Pacific and along the coast of the Eastern Suburbs. The Waverley Council still tends his grave as it does the graves of other district notabilities. Well might one echo the words of Horatio as Hamlet dropped dead:

'Now cracks a noble heart. Good night, sweet prince,
    And flights of angels sing thee to thy rest.'

Chronology

1877   2 November. Victor Trumper born, the eldest of eight children.

1894–5   He is one of 18 colts to play against A. D. Stoddart's First Team during the MCC visit to Australia. Scores 67 in that match but only 12th in the averages for the South Sydney Club.

1895   In his first appearance for New South Wales scores 11 and 0 at Adelaide against South Australia.

1896   Under Noble's influence, joins Paddington.

1897   Scores 5 and 0 for New South Wales against MCC but finishes season averaging 204·20 for Paddington.

1899   Scores 75 in the final trial against an Australian XI to win selection for the tour of England. During that tour scores 300 not out against Sussex at Hove and 135 not out at Lord's, his second Test innings.

1901–2   MacLaren's side tours Australia. Trumper's top score in Tests only 65.

1902   To England again with Darling's side. 2570 runs, 11 centuries in an appallingly wet summer. In October, tours South Africa, scoring 218 against Transvaal.

1903–4   MCC tour Australia and on 17 December at Sydney he scores a magnificent 185 against P. F. Warner's side.

1904   On 7 June marries Sarah Ann Briggs.

1905   Tours New Zealand, then England, where his best Test score is 31.

1907–8   MCC tour Australia, Trumper returning to form with 166 in the fifth Test.

1909–10   Makes his third tour of England, 73 in the Oval Test being his best score of the series. Also accompanies his parents to a new home in Help Street, Chatswood. South Africa tour Australia, and he scores 159 in the second Test, 214 not out in the third.

1911–12   MCC in Australia. Scores 113 in first Test.

1912   The 'Big Six' row. The effective end of Trumper's Test career against England.

1913   In February his testimonial raises £3000.

1914 His last great innings: in New Zealand in February
       scores 293 against Canterbury at Christchurch, in March
       211 against Southland.

1915 Dies on 28 June from Bright's Disease, aged 37.

VICTOR TRUMPER'S SCORES FOR N.S.W., AUSTRALIA AND 'REST OF AUSTRALIA'.

Don Bradman once asked one of Trumper's supporters: 'If he was everything you claim for him, why did he not score more runs for Australia?' That question was typical of Bradman, ever figure-conscious, but he was entitled to ask it. For the discrepancy in their scoring records, together with their relative performances on 'sticky' wickets, made up the two big differences in their careers.

In the following pages I reproduce both Trumper's and Bradman's first-class scores (the latter taken from Bradman's book *Farewell to Cricket*, Hodder and Stoughton, 1950), as many will wish to compare the two. Bradman's are by far the more imposing. He was much more consistent than Trumper, with an obviously sounder defence, and in his early days of success was dashing indeed; if in his later days his buccaneering batting was a little less conspicuous his consistency still remained. I wouldn't have thought any particular bowler would have got Bradman's wicket too often; if they had the batting wizard would have set out deliberately to destroy any suggestion of a bowler's superiority. But perhaps Alec Bedser, in England with his fine-leg trap, would have most qualified in England, while Bill O'Reilly, whom Bradman declared to be the best bowler in the world, the best qualified in Australia. Bill Andrews, a lovable, salty character, wrote a book, *The Hand that bowled Bradman*, but Bill didn't make it too clear that the Don had hit 202 before the title of the book came about!

In *Farewell to Cricket* Don Bradman writes: 'I do not want to enter into a discussion about Trumper (but does so immediately!) but perhaps, in fairness to myself, I may say this. If the argument is used that big scores were responsible for my high average then surely scores of up to 100 only would not come into it. In that regard Trumper's record in England disclosed 19 centuries in 193 innings, mine was 41 centuries in 120 innings. On a percentage basis, Trumper got one century for every 9.8 innings, whereas I obtained one century every 3.4.

'Perhaps I should also mention that my highest score against an English county is 258 compared with Trumper's 300 not out against Sussex on his first trip. These figures should successfully dispose of that contention. Further, I can find no merit in the action of any player who deliberately gets out when his side still requires runs.' There must have been more than a few times when the Don's run-glasses fogged up and he saw no glimmer of victory!

As I count them, Trumper got 25 ducks in first-class cricket and three in successive Test innings. That is an inordinate number of nils. Against that, Don Bradman got only fourteen in his very long career of 338 first-class innings, more than Trumper. It is to be noted how often Trumper was bowled and how often under double figures. If the Don got to double figures it usually meant a century; if to three figures, then on to double and treble centuries and often with a 'not out' tacked on. Rarely in first-class cricket did he ever get out in the nineties, and never in a Test. Nor did he clam up when he got near three figures, as many do. Bradman never messed about in the nineties: he sailed into the bowling with more gusto than ever.

The career analyses that follow prove conclusively that there was no comparison between the figures of the two Australian champions. Bradman wins by the length of the straight. It could be argued, and with much substance, I think, that Victor Trumper was not suited by the opening position, a proposition that his admirers will scoff at, no doubt, but he either took too many risks, as has been suggested, or he wasn't at all interested in playing safe against the new ball. Bradman loved to score off the very first ball, and often did, and one can hear again his shrill call of 'Right' echoing across a ground, but Trumper seemed to have his eyes set on hitting the first ball for four. Bradman rightly contends that runs are the name of the game; in judging batsmanship, however, equally important is how they are made.

TRUMPER'S RECORD SEASON BY SEASON

Match	First Innings	Second Innings
1894		
Eighteen Sydney Juniors v A. E. Stoddart's English team 21 & 23 Dec.	67	
1895		
New South Wales v South Australia (Adelaide) 5, 7, 8, 9 Jan.	run out 11	c Jones, b Giffen o
1897		
New South Wales v A. E. Stoddart's English Team 12, 13, 15, 16 Nov.	ct Ranjitsinhji, b Hirst 55	b Richardson o
1898		
New South Wales v South Australia (Adelaide) 8, 10, 11, 12 Jan.	c & b Giffen 48	b Jones 13
New South Wales v Victoria (Sydney) 22, 24, 25, 26, 27 Jan.	c & b McLeod 12	c Roche, b Trott 12
New South Wales v Stoddart's English Team (Sydney) 5, 7, 8, 9, 10, 11 Feb.	b Mason 4	b Hearne 23
New South Wales v South Australia (Sydney) 18, 19, 21, 22 Feb.	run out 68	st McKenzie, b Evans 7
New South Wales v Tasmania (Sydney) 9, 10, 12 Dec.	not out. 292	o
New South Wales v South Australia (Adelaide) 16, 17, 19, 20, 21 Dec.	c Jones, b Jarvis 68	c Jarvis, b Lyons o
New South Wales v Victoria (Melbourne) 23, 24, 26, 27 Dec.	c Graham, b McLeod 4	c Johns, b Trumble 19
1899		
New South Wales v South Australia (Sydney) 6, 7, 8, 9, 11 Jan.	c Jarvis, b Jones o	c Darling, b Jones 15

New South Wales v New Zealand (Sydney)

Match	1st innings		2nd innings	
26, 27, 28, 30 Jan.	c Trumble, b McLeod	23		
24, 25, 27 Feb.	lbw b Cobcroft	253		
Rest of Australia v Team for England 3, 4, 6, 7, 8 March (Sydney)	c Kelly, b Noble	6	run out	46
Rest of Australia v Team for England (Melbourne) 10, 11, 13 March	b McLeod	46	c & b Noble	26
Rest of Australia v Team for England (Adelaide) 17, 18, 20, 21 March	c Hill, b McLeod	75	b Trumble	0

10th AUSTRALIAN TEAM IN ENGLAND – 1899

Match	1st innings		2nd innings	
v Essex (Leyton) 11, 12, 13 May	b Young	0	b Young	3
v Surrey (Kennington Oval) 15, 16, 17 May	b Hayward	13		
v An England XI (Eastbourne) 12, 19, 20 May	run out	5	c Braybrooke, b Attewell	64
v Lancashire (Manchester) 25, 26 May	b Baker	82		
v Oxford University (Oxford) 29, 30, 31 May	b Stocks	25		
v England (Nottingham) 1st Test 1, 2, 3 June	b Hearne	0	b Jackson	11
v M.C.C. (Lord's) 5, 6, 7 June	b Grace	29		
v Cambridge University (Cambridge) 8, 9, 10 June	c Wilson, b Jessop	3		
v Yorkshire (Bradford) 12, 13, 14 June	c Hunter, b Hirst	21	b Hirst	19
v England (Lord's) 2nd Test	not out.	135		
v Oxford University Past and Present (Portsmouth)	c & b Forbes	55		

Match	First Innings	Second Innings
v Leicestershire (Leicester) 22, 23, 24 June	b Geeson · 12	
v Derbyshire (Derby) 26, 27, 28 June	lbw b Storer · 11	
v England (Leeds) 3rd Test 29, 30 June; 1 July	b Young · 12	c Ranjitsinhji, b Jackson · 32
v Notts (Nottingham) 3, 4, 5 July	c & b Attewell · 85	b Wass · 0
v An England XI (Truro) 7, 8 July	b Wilson · 19	
v Midland Counties XI (Birmingham) 10, 11, 12 July	c Lilley, b Arnold · 25	b Santall · 34
v Gloucestershire (Bristol) 13, 14, 15 July	b Roberts · 104	c & b Paish · 8
v England (Manchester) 4th Test 17, 18, 19 July	b Young · 14	b Hearne · 63
v Mr Grace's Team (Crystal Palace) 20, 21, 22 July	b Grace · 25	
v Surrey (Kennington Oval) 24, 25, 26 July	b Lockwood · 11	b Richardson · 68
v Sussex (Brighton) 27, 28, 29 July	not out · 300	
v M.C.C. and Ground (Lord's) 31 July; 1, 2 Aug.	b Trott · 4	
v Warwickshire (Birmingham) 7, 8, 9 Aug.	b Field · 0	not out · 9
v Kent (Canterbury) 10, 11, 12 Aug.	c Huish, b Du Boulay · 50	c Mason, b Bradley · 13
v England (Kennington Oval) 5th Test 14, 15, 16 Aug.	b Jones · 6	c & b Rhodes · 7
v Gloucestershire (Cheltenham) 17, 18, 19 Aug.	c & b Roberts · 1	b Paish · 2

Date	v Opponent	1st Innings		2nd Innings	
21, 22 Aug.		c MacGregor, b Trott	62		
	v Somerset (Taunton)				
24, 25, 26 Aug.		c Tyler, b Hedley	51		
	v Lancashire				
28, 29, 30 Aug.		c Ward, b Webb	10		
	v Mr C. I. Thornton's XI (Scarborough)				
31 Aug.; 1, 2 Sept.		c Storer, b Rhodes	14	st Storer, b Rhodes	12
	v South of England (Hastings)				
4, 5, 6 Sept.		c & b Jessop	25	c Board, b Bradley	2

TOUR AVERAGES (IN WHICH TRUMPER WAS PLACED 5th)

Matches	Innings	Runs	Most in an Innings	Not Out	Average
32	48	1556	300 not out	3	34.57

1899–1900 (IN AUSTRALIA)

Match	Date	1st Innings		2nd Innings	
New South Wales v South Australia (Adelaide)	16, 18, 19, 20 Dec. 1899	lbw b Giffen	165		
New South Wales v Victoria (Melbourne)	23, 26, 27, 28 Dec. 1899	c & b Trumble	57		
New South Wales v South Australia (Sydney)	9, 10, 11, 12 Jan. 1900	lbw b Giffen	45	c Hugo, b Jones	7
New South Wales v Victoria (Sydney)	26, 27, 29, 30, 31 Jan. 1900	hit wicket b Saunders	31	b Trumble	41
Australian XI v Rest of Australia	2, 3, 5, 6 Feb. 1900	c Jarvis, b Windsor	41	c Stuckey, b Windsor	49
New South Wales v Queensland (Sydney) 1899*		not out.	208		

1900–1 (IN AUSTRALIA)

Match	Date	1st Innings		2nd Innings	
New South Wales v South Australia (Adelaide)	17, 18, 19, 20 Dec. 1900	b Jarvis	32	lbw b Travers	53

* Dubious First Class

Match	First Innings		Second Innings	
New South Wales v Victoria (Melbourne) 24, 26, 27 Dec. 1900	c Graham, b Saunders	26	run out	26
New South Wales v South Australia (Sydney) 5, 7, 8, 9 Jan. 1901	b Jarvis	70		
New South Wales v Victoria (Sydney) 1, 2, 4, 5 Feb. 1901	c Saunders, b Trumble	21	c Ross, b Saunders	230

1901–2 (IN AUSTRALIA)

Match	First Innings		Second Innings	
New South Wales v South Australia (Sydney) 30 Nov.; 2, 3 Dec. 1901	c Hill, b Jones	21		
New South Wales v Victoria (Melbourne) 26, 27, 28, 30 Dec. 1901	b Armstrong	73	b Trumble	19
New South Wales v South Australia (Adelaide) 10, 11, 13, 14 Jan. 1902	c McKenzie, b Travers	5		

(v A. E. MacLaren's team 1901–2)

Match	First Innings		Second Innings	
For New South Wales (Sydney) 22, 23, 25, 26, 27 Nov. 1901	b Braund	67	b Braund	12
For Australia (Sydney) 1st Test 13, 14, 16 Dec. 1901	c & b Barnes	2	c Lilley, b Blythe	34
For Australia (Melbourne) 2nd Test 1, 2, 3, 4 Jan. 1902	b Barnes	0	c Lilley, b Barnes	16
For Australia (Adelaide) 3rd Test 17, 18, 20, 21, 22, 23 Jan. 1902	run out	65	b Gunn	25
For New South Wales (Sydney) 31 Jan.; 1, 3, 4, 5 Feb. 1902	lbw b Braund	35	c Lilley, b Jessop	35
For Australia (Sydney) 4th Test 14, 15, 17, 18 Feb. 1902	c Braund, b Jessop	7	lbw b Blythe	25
For Australia (Melbourne) 5th Test 28 Feb.; 1, 3, 4 March 1902	b Blythe	27	c McGahey, b Braund	18

AUSTRALIAN TEAM IN ENGLAND – 1902

Match	Date				
v [Londo]n County (Crystal Palace)	5, 6, 7 May	run out	9	st Board, b Braund	64
v Notts (Nottingham)	8, 9, 10 May	b Hallam	47		
v Surrey (Kennington Oval)	12, 13, 14 May	c Hayes, b Hayward	101		
v Essex (Leyton)	15, 16, 17 May	b Young	9		
v Leicestershire (Leicester)	19, 20, 21 May	b King	20		
v Oxford University (Oxford)	22, 23, 24 May	c Wild, b Evans	121		
v M.C.C. and Ground (Lord's)	26, 27, 28 May	b Hearne	105	b Trott	86
v England (Leeds)	29, 30, 31 May	b Hirst	18	c Braund, b Rhodes	14
v Yorkshire (Leeds)	2, 3 June	c Denton, b Jackson	38	b Hirst	7
v Lancashire (Manchester)	5, 6, 7 June	c MacLaren, b Sharp	70		
v Cambridge University (Cambridge)	9, 10 June	st Winter, b Dowson	128		
v England (Lord's) 1st Test	12, 13, 14 June	Washed out after first day			
v An England XI (Eastbourne)	16, 17, 18 June	b Bestwick	31	b Thompson	7
v Derbyshire (Derby)	19, 20, 21 June	c Humphries, b Bestwick	10		
v Yorkshire (Bradford)	23, 24 June	c Hirst, b Rhodes	3	c Hunter, b Rhodes	9
v An England XI (Bradford)	26, 27, 28 June	b Knutton	113		
v England (Sheffield) 3rd Test	3, 4, 5 July	b Braund	1	c Lilley, b Jackson	62

Match	First Innings		Second Innings	
v Warwickshire (Birmingham) 7, 8, 9 July	b Field	45		
v Gloucestershire (Bristol) 14, 15, 16 July	c Jessop, b Roberts	92		
v Somerset (Taunton) 17, 18, 19 July	c Hardy, b Gill	5	lbw b Gill	5
v Surrey (Kennington Oval) 21, 22, 23 July	c Stedman, b Lockwood	85		
v England (Manchester) 4th Test 24, 25, 26 July	c Lilley, b Rhodes	104	c Braund, b Lockwood	3
v Essex (Leyton) 28, 29, 30 July	b Mead	109	lbw b Reeves	119
v Sussex (Brighton) 31 July; 1, 2 Aug.	b Relf	21		
v Hampshire (Southampton) 7, 8 Aug.	c sub, b Llewellyn	18		
v England (Kennington Oval) 5th Test 11, 12, 13 Aug.	b Hirst	42	run out	2
v M.C.C. and Ground (Lord's) 14, 15, 16 Aug.	c Smith, b Mead	29		
v Gloucestershire (Cheltenham) 18, 19, 20 Aug.	c Champain, b Jessop	125		
v Kent (Canterbury) 21, 22, 23 Aug.	lbw b Mason	15	run out	69
v Middlesex (Lord's) 25, 26, 27 Aug.	c Trott, b Hearne	69	b Wells	23
v Lancashire (Liverpool) 28, 29, 30 Aug.	c Stanning, b Littlewood	4	b Kermode	6
v Eleven Players of England (Harrogate) 1, 2, 3 Sept.	st Gaukrodger, b Vine	127		
v Mr C. I. Thornton's XI (Scarborough) 4, 5, 6 Sept.	lbw b Rhodes	62	lbw b Thompson	55

Match	1st innings		2nd innings	
8, 9, 10 Sept.	b Gill	16	c Mason, b Gill	120
v South of England (Bournemouth) 11, 12, 13 Sept.	c & b Arnold	10	c Woods, b Tate	6
v Players of England (Kennington Oval) 15, 16, 17 Sept.	c & b Rhodes	96		

AUSTRALIAN TEAM IN SOUTH AFRICA – 1902

Match	1st innings		2nd innings	
v South Africa (Johannesburg) 11, 13, 14 Oct.	c Rowe, b Llewellyn	63	b Taberer	37
v Fifteen of the Transvaal (Pretoria) 15, 16, 17 Oct.	not out.	218*	b Sinclair	9
v South Africa (Johannesburg) 18, 20, 21 Oct.	b Kotze	18	c Shalders, b Sinclair	13
v Fifteen of Natal (Durban) 25, 27, 28 October	b Lees	52*	c Nourse, b Volger	13
v Fifteen of Western Province (Capetown) 5, 6 Nov.	c Rowe, b Middleton	49*	c Anderson, b Rowe	19
v South Africa (Capetown) 8, 10, 11 Nov.	b Llewellyn	70	not out	38

* Not First Class

1902–3 IN AUSTRALIA FOR N.S.W.

Match	1st innings		2nd innings	
v South Australia (Adelaide) 19, 20, 22, 23 Dec. 1902	c Waters, b Travers	10	Hit wicket b Claxton	2
v Victoria (Melbourne) 26, 27, 29 Dec. 1902	c Noonan, b Laver	51	c Stuckey, b Laver	22
v South Australia (Sydney) 9, 10, 12, 13 Jan. 1903	c Travers, b Kirkwood	178		
v Victoria (Sydney) 26, 27, 28, 29 Jan. 1903	c Hastings, b Collins	130	c Hastings, b Collins	0
v Lord Hawke's M.C.C. Team March 1903	b Bosanquet	37		

1903–4 (In Australia)

v P. F. Warner's M.C.C. Team

Match	First Innings		Second Innings	
For New South Wales (Sydney)				
20, 21, 23 Nov. 1903	st Lilley, b Rhodes	46	c Braund, b Hirst	11
For Australia (Sydney) 1st Test				
11, 12, 14, 15, 16, 17 Dec. 1903	c Foster, b Arnold	1	not out	185
For Australia (Melbourne) 2nd Test				
1, 2, 4, 5 Jan. 1904	c Tyldesley, b Rhodes	74	c Relf, b Rhodes	35
For Australia (Adelaide) 3rd Test				
15, 16, 18, 19, 20 Jan. 1904	b Hirst	113	lbw b Rhodes	59
For New South Wales				
12, 13, 15 Feb. 1904	c Hayward, b Hirst	44	b Braund	5
For Australia (Sydney) 4th Test				
26, 27, 28 Feb.; 1, 2, 3 March 1904	b Braund	7	lbw b Arnold	12
For Australia (Melbourne) 5th Test				
5, 7, 8 March 1904	c & b Braund	88	b Hirst	0

Interstate Matches For N.S.W.

Match	First Innings		Second Innings	
v South Australia (Sydney)				
4, 5, 7, 8 Dec. 1903	c Newman, b Reedman	26		
v South Australia (Adelaide)				
19, 21, 22, 23, 24 Dec. 1903	c Hack, b Claxton	61	not out	6
v Victoria (Melbourne)				
26, 28, 29 30, 31 Dec. 1903	b Laver	43	st Monfries, b Trott	68
v Victoria (Sydney)				
25, 26, 27 Jan. 1904	c Fry, b Trott	53	not out	53

1904–5 (In Australia)

Interstate Matches for N.S.W.

v South Australia (Sydney)

v Victoria (Sydney)
27, 28, 30, 31 Jan.; 1 Feb. 1905 . . st Carkeek, b Giller . . 81   run out . . . 13

1905 (IN NEW ZEALAND – FOR AUSTRALIA)

Match	Date	Dismissal	Score	Dismissal	Score
v Auckland XV (Auckland)	10, 11, 13 Feb. 1905	c Lusk, b Hay	92		
v Wellington XV (Wellington)	17, 18, 20 Feb. 1905	c Brice, b Tucker	10		
v Canterbury (Christchurch)	24, 25, 27 Feb. 1905	c Boxhall, b Callaway	6	not out	87
v Otago (Dunedin)	3, 4 March 1905	c Graham, b Austin	87		
v New Zealand (Christchurch)	10, 11, 12 March 1905	c Graham, b Fisher	84		
v New Zealand (Wellington)	March 1905	c Manson, b Bennett	172		

FOR AUSTRALIA IN ENGLAND – 1905

Match	Date	Dismissal	Score	Dismissal	Score
v Gentlemen of England (Crystal Palace)	4, 5, 6 May	b Brearley	2	b Beldam	7
v Notts (Nottingham)	8, 9, 10 May	c Oates, b Wass	0	c Oates, b Gunn	61
v Surrey (Kennington Oval)	11, 12, 13 May	lbw b Lees	31	b Lees	25
v Oxford University (Oxford)	15, 16, 17 May	c Carlisle, b Udal	77	b Udal	45
v Gentlemen of England (Lord's)	18, 19, 20 May	b Brearley	6		
v Yorkshire (Sheffield)	22, 23, 24 May	c Tunnicliffe, b Jackson	85	c Rhodes, b Haigh	8
v Lancashire (Manchester)	25, 26, 27 May	c Findlay, b Kermode	36	b Brearley	14
v England (Nottingham) 1st Test	29, 30, 31 May	retired hurt	13	absent hurt	0

Match	First Innings		Second Innings	
v Leicestershire (Leicester)				
12, 13, 14 June	c Knight, b Jayes	14	b Odell	70
v England (Lord's) 2nd Test				
15, 16, 17 June	b Jackson	31		
v Dublin University Past and Present (Dublin)				
19, 20, 21 June	lbw b Lynch	22	lbw b Meldon	65
v Warwickshire (Birmingham)				
26, 27, 28 June	c Lilley, b Hargreave	31		
v Gloucestershire (Bristol)				
29, 30 June; 1 July	c Townsend, b Brown	108		
v England (Leeds) 3rd Test				
3, 4, 5 July	b Warren	8	c Hirst, b Warren	0
v Hampshire (Southampton)				
6, 7, 8 July	c Johnston, b Persse	92		
v Derbyshire (Derby)				
10, 11, 12 July	b Morton	58	b Hunter	17
v Somerset (Bath)				
13, 14, 15 July	c Palairet, b Robson	86		
v Scotland (Edinburgh)				
17, 18, 19 July	c Jupp, b Anderson	15	c Dalmeny, b Peel	55
v Fifteen of Scotland (Glasgow)				
20, 21, 22 July	lbw b Nixon	30	c Nixon, b Smith	14
v England (Manchester) 4th Test				
24, 25, 26 July	c Rhodes, b Brearley	11	lbw b Rhodes	30
v Surrey (Kennington Oval)				
27, 28, 29 July	b Nice	13	lbw b Smith	35
v Sussex (Brighton)				
31 July; 1, 2 Aug.	c Butt, b Dwyer	17		
v Worcestershire (Worcester)				
3, 4, 5 Aug.	b Wilson	110		
v Middlesex (Lord's)				
10, 11, 12 Aug.	c Trott, b Beldam	0	c & b Trott	32

Match	Dates				
v Northamptonshire (Northampton)	14, 15, 16 Aug.	b Brearley	4	c Spooner, b Brearley	28
	17, 18, 19 Aug.	c (sub) b Driffield	68		
v Lancashire (Liverpool)	21, 22 Aug.	b Cook.	89		
v Kent (Canterbury)	24, 25, 26 Aug.	lbw b Mason	59		
v Gloucestershire (Cheltenham)	28, 29, 30 Aug.	b Jessop	27	c Godsell, b Jessop	29
v An XI of England (Bournemouth)	31 Aug.; 1, 2 Sept.	c Quaife, b Hargreave	52	lbw b Braund	30
v Essex (Leyton)	4, 5, 6 Sept.	b Tremlin	18	lbw b Douglas	11
v Mr C. I. Thornton's England XI (Scarborough)	7, 8, 9 Sept.	lbw b Rhodes	9		

1905–6 (IN AUSTRALIA FOR N.S.W.)

Match	Dates				
v South Australia (Sydney)	5, 6, 8, 9, 10 Jan. 1906	c Jarvis, b Reedman	16	c Hack, b Reedman	35
v Victoria (Sydney)	26, 27, 29, 30 Jan. 1906	b Saunders	101	b Christian.	23

1906–7 (IN AUSTRALIA – FOR N.S.W.)

Match	Dates		
v Victoria (Sydney)	25, 26, 28 Jan. 1907	c McAlister, b Saunders	11

1907

Match	Dates				
v Rest of Australia (Sydney) (For S.E. Gregory's Benefit)	15, 16, 18 Feb.	c Bowden, b Wright	9	c Bowden, b Hazlitt	3

M.C.C. IN AUSTRALIA – 1907–8

Match	Dates				
New South Wales v M.C.C. (Sydney)	22, 23, 25 Nov.	c Braund, b Blythe	38	c Braund, b Fiedler	6

Match	First Innings		Second Innings	
Australia v M.C.C. (Sydney) 1st Test				
13, 14, 16, 17, 18, 19 Dec.	b Fielder	43	b Barnes	3
Australia v M.C.C. (Melbourne) 2nd Test				
1, 2, 3, 4, 6 Jan.	c Humphries, b Crawford	49	lbw b Crawford	63
Australia v M.C.C. (Adelaide) 3rd Test				
10, 11, 13, 14, 15, 16 Jan.	b Fielder	4	b Barnes	0
Australia v M.C.C. (Melbourne) 4th Test				
7, 8, 10, 11 Feb.	c Crawford, b Fielder	0	b Crawford	0
New South Wales v M.C.C. (Sydney)				
14, 15, 17, 18, 19, 20 Feb.	b Blythe	14	c Jones, b Hardstaff	74
Australia v M.C.C. (Sydney) 5th Test				
21, 22, 24, 25, 26, 27 Feb.	c Braund, b Barnes	10	c Gunn, b Rhodes	166

INTER-STATE MATCHES 1907–8

Match	First Innings		Second Innings	
New South Wales v South Australia (Sydney)				
6, 7, 9, 10, 11, 12 Dec.	b Claxton	44	c Chamberlain, b Wright	135
New South Wales v Victoria (Melbourne)				
26, 27, 28, 30, 31 Dec.	c McAlister, b Saunders	29	c Collins, b Tarrant	119

1908
M.A. NOBLE'S TESTIMONIAL MATCH

Match	First Innings	
Australia XI v Rest of Australia (Sydney)		
20, 21, 23, 24 March	c Collins, b Laver	0

1909

Match	First Innings	
Australia XI v Rest of Australia (Sydney)		
5, 6, 8, 9 Feb.	c Gorry, b Saunders	0

FOR AUSTRALIA IN ENGLAND – 1909

Match	First Innings	
Australia v Notts (Nottingham)		
6, 7, 8 May	b Hallam	94
Australia v Northamptonshire (Northampton)		

Match	1st innings		2nd innings	
13, 14, 15 May.	c Fane, b Lees	74		
Australia v Surrey (Kennington Oval)				
17, 18, 19 May.	b Lees	2	c Hayes, b Crawford	20
Australia v M.C.C. (Lord's)				
20, 21, 22 May.	b Buckenham	0	b Buckenham	34
Australia v Oxford University (Oxford)				
24, 25, 26 May.	b Gilbert	2		
Australia v England (Birmingham) 1st Test				
27, 28, 29 May.	c Hirst, b Blythe	10	c Rhodes, b Hirst	1
Australia v Leicestershire (Leicester)				
31 May; 1, 2 June	run out	23	not out	26
Australia v Cambridge University (Cambridge)				
3, 4, 5 June	c Tufnell, b MacLeod	133		
Australia v Hampshire (Southampton)				
7, 8 June.	b Newman	9	c Newman, b Llewellyn	4
Australia v Somerset (Bath)				
10, 11, 12 June	b Robson	2	c Braund, b Robson	0
Australia v England (Lord's) 2nd Test				
14, 15, 16 June	c MacLaren, b Relf	28		
Australia v Lancashire and Yorkshire (Manchester) 24, 25, 26 June	c Hornby, b Rhodes	10		
Australia v Scotland (Edinburgh)				
28, 29 June	b Broadbent	8	run out	3
Australia v England (Leeds) 3rd Test				
1, 2, 3 July	not out.	27	b Barnes	2
Australia v Warwickshire (Birmingham)				
5, 6, 7 July	b Foster	1		
Australia v Worcestershire (Worcester)				
8, 9, 10 July	b Cuffe	7		
Australia v Gloucestershire (Bristol)				
12, 13, 14 July	b Rattenbury	25		
Australia v Surrey (Kennington Oval)				
15, 16, 17 July	lbw b Lees	25	st Strudwick, b Smith	0

Match	First Innings		Second Innings	
Australia v Yorkshire (Sheffield)				
19, 20, 21 July	c Hunter, b Newstead	5		
Australia v Derbyshire (Derby)				
22, 23, 24 July	c Humphries, b Morton	113		
Australia v England (Manchester) 4th Test				
26, 27, 28 July	c Hutchings, b Barnes	2	c Tyldesley, b Rhodes	48
Australia v Lancashire (Liverpool)				
5, 6, 7 Aug.	b Dean	8	b Dean	54
Australia v England (Kennington Oval) 5th Test				
9, 10, 11 Aug.	c Rhodes, b Barnes	73	st Lilley, b Carr	20
Australia v An England XI (Blackpool)				
12, 13, 14 Aug.	c V. Crawford, b Jayes	49	b Reeves	150
Australia v Gloucestershire (Cheltenham)				
16, 17, 18 Aug.	c Board, b Dennett	48		
Australia v Kent (Canterbury)				
19, 20, 21 Aug.	c Humphreys, b Woolley	20		
Australia v Sussex (Brighton)				
26, 27, 28 Aug.	b Vincett	31	c Smith, b Killick	25
Australia v M.C.C. (Lord's)				
30, 31 Aug.; 1 Sept.	b Fielder	80		
Australia v Essex (Leyton)				
2, 3, 4 Sept.	c Carpenter, b Young	71		
Australia v Mr Bamford's XI (Uttoxeter)				
6, 7, 8 Sept.	c Hayes, b Barnes	12		

IN AUSTRALIA – 1909–10
(Trumper did not play in Sheffield Shield matches)

1910
SHEFFIELD SHIELD FOR NEW SOUTH WALES

Match	First Innings		Second Innings	
New South Wales v Rest of Australia (Sydney)				
21, 22, 24, 25 Jan.	c O'Connor, b Armstrong	105		
New South Wales v South Africa (Sydney)			at Sherwell, b Faullmer	78

. . . 2, 3, 3, 8 Dec.	c Moyle, b Whitty	75	b Whitty	0
Australia v South Africa (Sydney) 9, 10, 12, 13, 14 Dec.	run out	27		
New South Wales v Victoria (Melbourne) 24, 26, 27, 28 Dec.	b Kyle	52	c Matthews, b Ransford	142

1910–11

MATCHES v SOUTH AFRICA

Australia v South Africa (Melbourne) 31 Dec.; 2, 3, 4 Jan.	b Pegler	34	b Faulkner	159
Australia v South Africa (Adelaide) 7, 9, 10, 11, 12, 13 Jan.	not out	214	b Llewellyn	28

SHEFFIELD SHIELD FOR NEW SOUTH WALES

New South Wales v Victoria (Sydney) 27, 28, 30, 31 Jan.	b Laver	4	c Healy, b Kyle	82

MATCHES v SOUTH AFRICA

For Australia v South Africa (Melbourne) 17, 18, 20, 21 Feb.	b Faulkner	7	c Sherwell, b Vogler	87
For New South Wales v South Africa (Sydney) 24, 25, 27, 28 Feb.; 1 March	b Pearse	5	b Sinclair	15
For Australia v South Africa (Sydney) 3, 4, 6, 7 March	b Schwarz	31	not out	74
For Australian XI v Rest of Australia (Melbourne) 17, 18, 20 March	b Noble	62		

FOR NEW SOUTH WALES IN SHEFFIELD SHIELD MATCHES

New South Wales v South Australia (Sydney) 1, 2, 4, 5, 6 Dec.	b Whitty	47	c Stirling, b Whitty	37
New South Wales v Victoria (Melbourne) 23, 26, 27 Dec.	c Hartkopf, b Matthews	58		

Match	First Innings		Second Innings	
v M.C.C. Team				
For New South Wales v M.C.C. (Sydney) 24, 25, 27, 28 Nov.	c Strudwick, b Foster .	1		
For an Australian XI v M.C.C. (Brisbane) 8, 9, 11 Dec.	c Hearne, b Iremonger .	30		
1911				
For Australia v M.C.C. (Sydney) 1st Test 15, 16, 18, 19, 20, 21 Dec.	c Hobbs, b Woolley .	113	c & b Douglas .	14
1911–12				
For Australia v M.C.C. (Melbourne) 2nd Test 30 Dec.; 1, 2, 3 Jan.	b Foster .	13	b Barnes .	2
New South Wales v South Australia (Adelaide) 6, 8, 9, 10 Jan.	not out.	21	not out	13
For Australia v M.C.C. (Adelaide) 3rd Test 12, 13, 15, 16, 17 Jan.	b Hitch .	26	not out	1
For New South Wales v M.C.C. (Sydney) 5th Test 23, 24, 26, 27, 28, 29 Feb.; 1 March	c Woolley, b Barnes .	5	c Woolley, b Barnes .	50
New South Wales v South Australia (Adelaide) 20, 21, 23 Dec.	b Whitty .	0	b Whitty .	11
New South Wales v Victoria (Melbourne) 26, 27, 28 Dec.	c & b Matthews .	25	c Carkeek, b McNaughton .	10
1913				
New South Wales v South Australia (Sydney) 10, 11, 13, 14 Jan.	not out.	201	b Whitty .	25
New South Wales v Victoria (Sydney) 24, 25, 27, 28 Jan.	b Matthews .	138		
For New South Wales v Rest of Australia (Sydney) (Victor Trumper's Benefit Match)				

19, 20, 22, 23 Dec. . . c Steele, b Kirkwood . . 20 b Crawford 18

1914

New South Wales v New Zealand (Sydney)
26, 27 Dec. . . . b Sandman . . 32
New South Wales v Victoria (Sydney)
23, 24, 26, 27, 28 Jan. . c Armstrong, b Lugton . 24

1914 IN NEW ZEALAND – FOR A. SIM'S AUSTRALIAN TEAM
(Not all details are available)

v Wanganui (Wanganui)
24, 25 Feb. . . c Hussey, b Bernau . . 94
v Canterbury (Christchurch)
27, 28 Feb.; 2 March . c Sandman, b Bennett . . 292
v South Canterbury (Temuka)
3, 4 March . . b Thomas . . . 135
v New Zealand (Dunedin)
6, 7, 9 March . . c Bennett, b Sandman . . 72
v Southland (Invercargill)
10, 11 March . . c J. Hamilton, b Bannerman . 211
v Nelson (Nelson)
18, 19 March . . b Neale . . . 54
v Wellington (Wellington)
20, 21 March . . c Saunders, b Gibbes . . 67
v Manawatu (Palmerston North)
23, 24 March . . c Luxford, b McVicar . . 76
v New Zealand (Auckland)
27, 28, 30 March . . lbw b Sneddon . . 81

1916

For Australia v M.C.C. (Melbourne) 4th Test
9, 10, 12, 13 Feb. . . b Foster . . . 17 b Barnes . . . 28

Match	First Innings		Second Innings	
1927–8 (IN AUSTRALIA)				
New South Wales v South Australia	c Williams, b Scott	118	b Grimmett	33
New South Wales v Victoria	lbw, b Hartkoph	31	b Blackie	5
New South Wales v Queensland	b Gough	0	c O'Connor, b Nothling	13
New South Wales v South Australia	c & b McKay	2	st Hack, b Grimmett	73
New South Wales v Victoria	st Ellis, b Blackie	7	Not out	134
1928–9 (IN AUSTRALIA)				
New South Wales v M.C.C.	b Freeman	87	not out	132
An Australian XI v M.C.C.	not out	58	lbw, b Tate	18
Australia v England	lbw, b Tate	18	c Chapman, b White	1
Australia v England	b Hammond	79	c Duckworth, b Geary	112
Australia v England	c Larwood, b Tate	40	run out	58
Australia v England	c Tate, b Geary	123	not out	37
New South Wales v M.C.C.	c Tyldesley, b White	15		
The Rest v Australia	c Oldfield, b Grimmett	14	b Oxenham	5
New South Wales v Queensland	c O'Connor, b Thurlow	131	not out	133
New South Wales v Victoria	b Hendry	1	not out	71
New South Wales v South Australia	c Grimmett, b Wall	5	b Wall	2
New South Wales v Victoria	not out	340		
New South Wales v South Australia	c Walker, b Grimmett	35	c Walker, b Carlton	175
1929–30 (IN AUSTRALIA)				
New South Wales v M.C.C.	b Worthington	157		
Trial Match	c Jackson, b Oxenham	124	lbw, b Grimmett	225
New South Wales v Queensland	run out	48	c O'Connor, b Brew	66
New South Wales v South Australia	run out	2	lbw, b Grimmett	84
New South Wales v Victoria	b Alexander	89	not out	26
New South Wales v Queensland	c Leeson, b Hurwood	3	not out	452
New South Wales v South Australia	c Richardson, b Whitfield	47		
New South Wales v Victoria	c Ellis, b Ironmonger	77		

Match	Dismissal	Score	Dismissal	Score
1930 Australian XI v Tasmania	c Kushforth, b Atkinson	139		
1930 Australian XI v Western Australia	c R. Bryant, b Evans	27		

1930 (IN ENGLAND)

Match	Dismissal	Score	Dismissal	Score
Australians v Worcester	c Walters, b Brook	236		
Australians v Leicester	not out	185		
Australians v Yorkshire	c & b Macauley	78		
Australians v Lancashire	b McDonald	9	not out	48
Australians v M.C.C.	b Allom	66	lbw, b Stevens	4
Australians v Derby	c Elliott, b Worthington	44		
Australians v Surrey	not out	252		
Australians v Oxford University	b Garland-Wells	32		
Australians v Hampshire	c Mead, b Boyes	191		
Australians v Middlesex	b Hearne	35	b Stevens	18
Australians v Cambridge University	c Barnes, b Human	32		
Australia v England	b Tate	8	b Robins	131
Australians v Surrey	c Allom, b Shepherd	5		
Australians v Lancashire	c Duckworth, b Sibbles	38	not out	23
Australia v England	c Chapman, b White	254	c Chapman, b Tate	1
Australians v Yorkshire	lbw, b Robinson	1		
Australia v England	c Duckworth, b Tate	334		
Australia v England	c Duleepsinhji, b Peebles	14		
Australians v Somerset	c & b Young	117		
Australians v Glamorgan	b Ryan	58	not out	19
Australians v Northants	b Jupp	22	c Hawtin, b Cox	35
Australia v England	c Duckworth, b Larwood	232		
Australians v Gloucester	c Sinfield, b Parker	42	b Parker	14
Australians v Kent	lbw, b Freeman	18	not out	205
Australians v An England XI	lbw, b Allom	63		
Australians v Leveson-Gower's XI	b Parker	96		

1930–1 (IN AUSTRALIA)

Match	Dismissal	Score	Dismissal	Score
New South Wales v West Indians	c Barrow, b Francis	73	c Headley, b Martin	22

Match	First Innings		Second Innings	
New South Wales v West Indians	b Constantine	10	lbw, b Griffith	73
Australia v West Indies	c Grant, b Griffith	4		
Australia v West Indies	c Barrow, b Francis	25		
Australia v West Indies	c Grant, b Constantine	223		
Australia v West Indies	c Roach, b Martin	152		
Australia v West Indies	c Francis, b Martin	43	b Griffith	0
New South Wales v South Australia	c Pritchard, b Deverson	61	c Waite, b Deverson	121
New South Wales v South Australia	b Richardson	258		
New South Wales v Victoria	c Hendry, b a'Beckett	2		
New South Wales v Victoria	c Barnett, b Alexander	33	c Rigg, b Ironmonger	220
Woodfull's XI v Ryder's XI	b Mailey	73	c & b Mailey	29
1931–2 (In Australia)				
New South Wales v South Africans	c & b McMillan	30	c Bell, b Morkel	135
New South Wales v South Africans	c Curnow, b McMillan	219		
New South Wales v Queensland	c Waterman, b Gilbert	0		
New South Wales v Victoria	c Smith, b Ironmonger	23	b Nagel	167
New South Wales v South Australia	b Carlton	23	b Wall	0
Australia v South Africa	lbw, b Vincent	226		
Australia v South Africa	c Viljoen, b Morkel	112		
Australia v South Africa	c Cameron, b Quinn	2	lbw, b Vincent	167
Australia v South Africa	not out.	299		
1932–3 (In Australia)				
Combined XI v M.C.C.	c Hammond, b Verity	3	c Pataudi, b Allen	10
An Australian XI v M.C.C.	lbw, b Larwood	36	b Larwood	13
New South Wales v M.C.C.	lbw, b Tate	18	b Voce	23
Australia v England	b Bowes	0	not out	103
Australia v England	c Allen, b Larwood	8	c & b Verity	66
Australia v England	b Larwood	76	c Mitchell, b Larwood	24
Australia v England	b Larwood	48	b Verity	71
New South Wales v M.C.C.	b Mitchell	1	c Ames, b Hammond	71

Match	Dismissal	Score	Dismissal	Score
New South Wales v Victoria	c Bromley, b Ironmonger	157		97
New South Wales v South Australia	c Ryan, b Wall	56	b Lee	
1933–4 (In Australia)				
New South Wales v Queensland	c Andrews, b Levy	200		
New South Wales v South Australia	b Collins	1	st Walker, b Grimmett	76
New South Wales v Victoria	not out.	187	not out	77
New South Wales v Queensland	b Brew	253		
New South Wales v Victoria	c Darling, b Fleetwood-Smith	128		
Testimonial Match	c Woodfull, b Wall	55	c Darling, b Blackie	101
New South Wales v The Rest	c Walker, b Chilvers	22	b Ebeling	92
1934 (In England)				
Australians v Worcester	b Howarth	206		
Australians v Leicester	b Geary	65		
Australians v Cambridge University	b Davies	0		
Australians v M.C.C.	c & b Brown	5		
Australians v Oxford University	lbw, b Dyson.	37		
Australians v Hampshire	c Mead, b Baring	0		
Australians v Middlesex	c Hulme, b Peebles.	160		
Australians v Surrey	c Squires, b Gover	77		
Australia v England	c Hammond, b Geary	29	c Ames, b Farnes	25
Australia v England	c & b Verity	36	c Ames, b Verity	13
Australians v Northants	c Bakewell, b Matthews	65	b Matthews	25
Australians v Somerset	c Luckes, b White	17		
Australians v Surrey	c Brooks, b Holmes	27	not out	61
Australia v England	c Ames, b Hammond	30		
Australians v Derby	c Elliott, b Townsend	71	not out	6
Australians v Yorkshire	b Leyland	140		
Australia v England	b Bowes	304		
Australia v England	c Ames, b Bowes	244	b Bowes	77
Australians v Essex	b Pearce	19		
Australians v An English XI	not out.	149		
Australians v Leveson-Gower's XI	st Duckworth, b Verity	132		

| | First Innings | | Second Innings | |
Match				
1935–6 (In Australia)				
South Australia v M.C.C.	lbw, b Sims	15	lbw, b Parks	50
South Australia v New South Wales	c & b Robinson	117		
South Australia v Queensland	c Tallon, b Levy	233		
South Australia v Victoria	c Quin, b Bromley	357		
South Australia v Queensland	c Wyeth, b Gilbert	31		
South Australia v New South Wales	c Little, b Hynes	0		
South Australia v Tasmania	c & b Townley	369		
South Australia v Victoria	c Ledward, b Ebeling	1		
1936–7 (In Australia)				
An Australian XI v M.C.C.	b Worthington	63		
Australia v England	c Worthington, b Voce	38	c Fagg, b Allen	0
Australia v England	c Allen, b Voce	0	b Verity	82
Australia v England	c Robins, b Verity	13	c Allen, b Verity	270
South Australia v M.C.C.	c Ames, b Barnett	38		
Australia v England	b Allen	26	c & b Hammond	212
Australia v England	b Farnes	169		
South Australia v Victoria	c O'Brien, b Gregory	192		
South Australia v Queensland	st Tallon, b Wyeth	123		
South Australia v New South Wales	lbw, b O'Reilly	24	not out	38
South Australia v Victoria	c Ebeling, b Fleetwood-Smith	31	c Hassett, b McCormick	8
Testimonial Match	c O'Reilly, b Grimmett	212	c Fingleton, b Grimmett	13
1937–8 (In Australia)				
South Australia v New South Wales	c O'Brien, b O'Reilly	91	c Chipperfield, b O'Reilly	62
South Australia v Queensland	c Baker, b Dixon	246	not out	39
South Australia v Victoria	c Sievers, b Gregory	54	c Sievers, b Gregory	35
South Australia v Queensland	c Tallon, b Dixon	107	c Hackett, b Allen	113
South Australia v New South Wales	c McCabe, b O'Brien	44	not out	104
South Australia v Victoria	b McCormick	3	c Ledward, b Thorn	85
Testimonial Match	b Grimmett	17		
South Australia v West Australia	c Wilberforce, b Eyres	101		

Match				
1938 Australian XI v Tasmania	c Sankey, b Thomas	79		
1938 Australian XI v Tasmania	b Jeffrey	144		
1938 Australian XI v Western Australia	st Lovelock, b Zimbulis	102		

1938 (In England)

Match				
Australians v Worcester	c Martin, b Howarth	258		
Australians v Oxford University	lbw, b Evans	58		
Australians v Cambridge University	c Mann, b Wild	137		
Australians v M.C.C.	c Robins, b Smith	278		
Australians v Northants	c James, b Partridge	2		
Australians v Surrey	c Brooks, b Watts	143		
Australians v Hampshire	not out.	145		
Australians v Middlesex	c Compton, b Nevell	5	not out	30
Australia v England	c Ames, b Sinfield	51	not out	144
Australians v Gentlemen	c Valentine, b Meyer	104		
Australians v Lancashire	c Pollard, b Phillipson	12	not out	101
Australia v England	b Verity	18	not out	102
Australians v Yorkshire	st Wood, b Smailes	59	c Barber, b Smailes	42
Australians v Warwickshire	c Wilmot, b Mayer	135		
Australians v Notts	lbw, b Jepson	56	c Jepson, b Marshall	144
Australia v England	b Bowes	103	c Verity, b Wright	16
Australians v Somerset	b Andrews	202		
Australians v Glamorgan	st H. Davies, b Clay	17		
Australians v Kent	c Todd, b Watt	67		

1938–9 (In Australia)

Match		
M.C.C. Centenary Match	b Nagel	118
South Australia v New South Wales	b Murphy	143
South Australia v Queensland	c Baker, b Christ	225
South Australia v Victoria	c Hassett, b Sievers	107
South Australia v Queensland	c Christ, b W. Tallon	186
South Australia v New South Wales	not out.	135
South Australia v Victoria	c Fleetwood-Smith, b Thorn	5

1939–40 (IN AUSTRALIA)

Match	First Innings		Second Innings	
South Australia v Victoria	run out.	76	lbw, b Ring	64
South Australia v New South Wales	not out.	251	not out	90
South Australia v Queensland	c Hansen, b Ellis	138		
South Australia v Victoria	c Johnson, b Fleetwood-Smith	267		
South Australia v Queensland	c Dixon, b Stackpoole	0	c Tallon, b Cook.	97
South Australia v New South Wales	lbw, b O'Reilly	39	c sub, b Pepper	40
South Australia v West Australia	c Lovelock, b MacGill	42	not out	209
South Australia v West Australia	c Zimbulis, b Eyres.	135		
Rest of Australia v New South Wales	c Saggers, b O'Reilly	25	c McCool, b Cheetham	2

1940–1 (IN AUSTRALIA)

Match	First Innings		Second Innings	
South Australia v Victoria	c Sievers, b Dudley	0	b Sievers	6
Patriotic Match	c Tamblyn, b Ellis	0	b O'Reilly	12

1945–6 (IN AUSTRALIA)

Match	First Innings		Second Innings	
South Australia v Queensland	c Tallon, b McCool	68	not out	52
South Australia v Services Team	c Carmody, b Williams	112		

1946–7 (IN AUSTRALIA)

Match	First Innings		Second Innings	
South Australia v M.C.C.	c & b Smith	76	c Edrich, b Pollard	3
An Australian XI v M.C.C.	c Pollard, b Compton	106		
South Australia v Victoria	st Baker, b Johnson.	43	st Baker, b Tribe.	119
Australia v England	b Edrich	187		
Australia v England	lbw, b Yardley	234		
Australia v England	b Yardley	79	c & b Yardley	49
Australia v England	b Bedser	0	not out	56
Australia v England	b Wright	12	c Compton, b Bedser	63
South Australia v M.C.C.	c Langridge, b Wright	5		

1947–8 (IN AUSTRALIA)

Match	First Innings		Second Innings	
South Australia v Indians	c Sarwate, b Mankad	156	st Sen, b Mankad.	12

Match	1st Innings		2nd Innings	
An Australian XI v Indians		172	c Sarwate, b Mankad	26
Australia v India	hit wicket, b Amarnath	185		
Australia v India	b Hazare	13		
Australia v India	lbw, b Phadkar	132	not out	127
Australia v India	b Hazare	201		
Australia v India	retired hurt	57		
1948 Australian XI v Western Australia	c Outridge, b O'Dwyer	115		

1948 (IN ENGLAND)

Match	1st Innings		2nd Innings	
Australians v Worcester	b Jackson	107		
Australians v Leicester	c Corrall, b Etherington	81		
Australians v Surrey	b Bedser	146		
Australians v Essex	b P. Smith	187		
Australians v M.C.C.	c Edrich, b Deighton	98		
Australians v Lancashire	b Hilton	11	st E. Edrich, b Hilton	43
Australians v Notts	b Woodhead	86		
Australians v Sussex	b Cornford	109		
Australia v England	c Hutton, b Bedser	138	c Hutton, b Bedser	0
Australians v Yorkshire	c Yardley, b Wardle	54	c Hutton, b Aspinall	86
Australia v England	c Hutton, b Bedser	38	c Edrich, b Bedser	89
Australians v Surrey	c Barton, b Squires	128		
Australia v England	lbw, b Pollard	7	not out	30
Australians v Middlesex	c Compton, b Whitcombe	6		
Australia v England	b Pollard	33	not out	173
Australians v Derby	b Gothard	62		
Australians v Warwickshire	b Hollies	31	not out	13
Australians v Lancashire	c Wilson, b Roberts	28	not out	133
Australia v England	b Hollies	0		
Australians v Kent	c Valentine, b Crush	65		
Australians v Gentlemen	c Donnelly, b Brown	150		
Australians v South of England	c Mann, b Bailey	143		
Australians v Leveson-Gower's XI	c Hutton, b Bedser	153		

1948–9 (IN AUSTRALIA)

Match				First Innings	Second Innings
Bradman Testimonial	.	.	.	c Harvey, b Dooland . 123	c Saggers, b Johnson . . 10
Oldfield-Kippax Testimonial	.	.	.	c Meuleman, b Miller . 53	
South Australia v Victoria	.	.	.	b W. Johnston . 30	

NATURE OF BRADMAN'S DISMISSALS

Bowled . .	78
Caught by fieldsman . .	121
Caught and bowled . .	12
Caught by wicket-keeper .	40
Stumped . . .	12
Run out . .	4
Leg before wicket . .	27
Hit wicket . .	1
Not out . .	43
	338

INDEX

Abel, R., 80, 133, 134
Adelaide, 55, 61, 62, 63, 66, 84, 85, 91, 107, 111, 124, 140, 141, 145, 150
Altham, H. S., 34, 36, 40, 169
America, 128, 129, 133, 148
Arlott, L. T. J., 40
Armstrong, W. W., 79, 81, 83, 116, 122, 123, 138, 139, 142, 144, 145, 147, 153, 160, 161
Arnold, E., 117
Ashley-Cooper, F. S., 70, 71
Atfield, A. J., 133
Australasian, The, 46, 144
Australian Cricket Annual of 1896, 56
Australian Cricket Board of Control, 111, 127, 142, 143, 144, 145, 147, 150, 151
Ayres, F. H., 168

Bailey, Sir Abe, 133
Baker, 'Snowy', 170
Ballarat, 45
Balmain C.C., 26, 78
Bannerman, A. C., 55
Bannerman, C., 55, 58, 59
Barbour, E. P., 32, 55, 153f
Barbour, G., 55
Bardsley, W., 138f, 142, 153, 167, 171
Barker, Ralph, 38
Barnes, S. F., 82, 114
Barry and Morris, 157
Bean, E. E., 144
Bean, G., 133
Beauclerk, Rev. Lord F., 127
Beldham, G. W., 102
Beldham, W., 128, 168
Bell, F. W., 132
Bell's Life, 130
Benaud, R., 103, 149
Bennett, J. H., 160, 162
Birmingham (*see* Edgbaston)
Blackham, J. McC., 75, 84, 85
Boer War, Second, 83, 141
Bosanquet, B. J. T., 30, 31, 117, 122, 124, 140
Bournemouth, 82
Bowden, S. H., 58
Bowden, Mr, 156
Box, C., 44

Boycott, G., 64, 151
Boys' Own Paper, 57
Bradley, W. M., 73
Bradman, Sir D. G., 21, 32f, 42, 64, 68, 77, 87, 101, 102, 107f, 126, 147, 167f
Braund, L. C., 80, 82, 113f, 121
Brave New World, 152
Brearley, W., 168
Briggs, J., 55, 73, 133
Briggs, Sarah Ann (*see* Trumper, Mrs Victor)
Brighton, 70, 71
Brisbane, 34, 79, 91, 101, 102, 125, 139, 147
Bristol, 73
Broken Hill, 86
Broomfield, Colonel, 47
Buchan family, the, 160
Bulli, 56
Burton Joyce, 129
Burwood C.C., 64
Butler, F., 133
Byron, Lord, 22

Caesar, Julius, 29, 134
Caffyn, W., 131, 133
Cambridge University C.C., 35, 46, 72, 74
Canada, 47, 129
Canberra, 148, 168
Canterbury (New Zealand), 160, 161
Cape Town, 84
Cardus, Sir Neville, 79, 87, 109, 114, 131, 132
Carlton, 56, 58
Carter, H., 32, 34, 55, 83, 111, 123, 125, 142, 145, 147, 153, 156, 171
Caruso, Enrico, 29
Central Cumberland C.C., 64
Champion, F. H. B., 70, 74
Chapman, W. W., 90
Chappell, G. S., 63, 69, 109, 147, 151
Chappell, I., 111, 126, 147
Chatswood, 57, 58, 167f
Checkett, C., 61
Christchurch (New Zealand), 159f
Clarke, William, 128
Clayton, H. J. R., 155

Cody, L. A., 160, 161
Collins, H. L., 92, 153, 155, 159, 160
Columbus, Christopher, 29
Commaille, M., 140
Connell, Mr, 64
Corbett, C., 108, 109
Cornwall, 71
Cosier, Mr, 149
Cotter, A., 55, 141, 142, 145, 147, 167, 171
Coughlan, Miss Louise (*see* Trumper, Mrs Charles)
Cowdrey, M. C., 168
Cranswick, Rev. E. H., 171
Crawford, J. N., 153, 160, 161
Creswick, Mr, 64
Cricket and Cricketers, 21
Cricket Crisis, 107, 108
Cricket is My Life, 78
Cricket Under Fire, 77
Cricketers' Club of Sydney, 26
Cricketers' Fund Friendly Society, 136
Crockett, R., 117, 119, 120, 121, 124
Crouch, G. S., 144, 145
Crown Street Superior Public School, 52, 54, 57, 170
Crystal Palace, 34, 70

Daily Mail, 120
Daily Telegraph, 35
Darcy, L., 41
Darling, D. K., 66, 142
Darling, Hon. J., 21, 65, 66, 70f, 81, 83, 86, 111, 113, 124, 142, 143, 145, 149
Darling, L. S., 111
Darlinghurst, 19, 49, 169
Davidson, A. K., 168
Davidson, G., 136
Davis Cup, 49
Davis, J. C., 56, 87, 90, 91, 92, 115f, 171
Derbyshire C.C.C., 136
Dickens, Charles, 128, 169
Dickens, Sir Henry, 169
Dingley Dell, 128
Dodge, Mr, 125
Dolling, Dr C. E., 144, 160
Donoghue, Mr, 64
Dorset, Duke of, 127
Douglas, J. W. H. T., 170
Dreyfus, Captain, 69
Duff, R. A., 40, 55, 80, 83, 95, 113, 117, 118, 138, 139
Durban, 84, 133

Dwyer, E. A., 38, 39

Eastbourne, 68
Edgbaston, 71, 82
80 Not Out, 55
Elliott, C. S., 121
England v Australia (Barker and Rosenwater), 38
Essex C.C.C., 68, 75, 170
Evans, E., 58

Farewell to Cricket, 36
Faulkner, G. A., 138, 139, 140
Fender, P. G. H., 35, 36
Fenner's, 131
Ferguson, W. H., 162
Ferrier, T., 92, 93
Fiji, 142
Fingleton, Jacquelyn, 41
Fingleton, J. H., 148
Fletcher, J. W., 90, 109, 110, 112
Foster, F. R., 112, 114, 147
Foster, R. E., 70, 113f, 121, 123
Foxton, Colonel, 144
Frederick the Great, 22
Fry, C. B., 21, 57, 71, 73, 79, 82, 102, 105, 106, 109, 112, 123
Fry's Magazine, 57
Fusedale, R., 170

Gadshill Place, 169
Gallipoli Campaign, 145
Game's the Thing, The, 95
Garrett, T. W., 57, 156
Gascoigne, Mr, 30, 91, 92, 170
Gee, Mr, 92
Ghers, D. R. A., 139, 140
Giffen, G., 61, 62, 63, 84f
Giltinan, J. J., 125
Gipps, Sir G., 47
Glebe C.C., 64
Glossop family, the, 164
Gloucestershire C.C.C., 35, 73, 74
Goddard, H., 29
Gordons C.C., 25, 41, 170
Grace, Dr E. M., 45
Grace, Dr W. G., 21, 24, 34, 35, 37, 38, 70, 76, 85, 86, 91, 100, 109, 128, 168
Great Batsmen: Their Methods at a Glance, 103
Great War, First, 74
Gregory, S. E., 57, 65, 69, 70, 72, 79, 80, 116, 117, 118, 142, 171
Greig, A. W., 137, 150, 151

Grimmett, C. V., 54
Guardian (Sydney), 147, 148
Gunn, W., 134, 137

Haigh, S., 82
Hamilton, Duke of, 127
Hamlet, 171
Hammersley, W. J., 46
Hammond, W. R., 104, 107, 137
Hampden Oval Cricket Ground (*see* Trumper Park)
Hampden, Viscount, 50
Hannaford, R., 168
Hannibal, 22
Harris, Lord, 135
Harrogate, 148, 151
Hartley, H. Haigh, 59
Hassett, A. L., 38
Hawke, Lord, 82, 135, 136
Hayes, C., 31
Hayward, T. W., 36, 62, 68, 73, 121, 134, 168
Headingley, 73
Hearne, F., 133
Hearne, J. T., 38, 68
Hearne, Walter, 134, 135
Hendren, E., 168
Hill, Clement, 72, 73, 78, 79, 80, 81, 83, 102, 113f, 138f, 153
Hill, L., 55
Hirst, G. H., 32, 33, 62, 82, 117, 118, 123, 124, 168
History of Cricket, A (Altham and Swanton), 34
Hobbs, Sir J. B., 21, 33f, 109, 137, 168
Holland, 44
Hook, J., 167
Hopkins, A. J., 83, 123
Horatio, 171
Hordern, H. V., 153, 171
Houghton, T. J., 155f
Howell, W. P., 64, 80, 83, 117, 123
Hucknall, 129
Hugo, V., 84
Hunter, J., 92, 93
Hutton, Sir L., 78, 137
Huxley, A., 152

Illingworth, R., 137
Imperial Cricket Conference, 87
India, 133, 137, 150
Institute of Aboriginal Affairs, 168
Invercargill, 162

Iredale, F. A., 18, 24, 25, 70, 120, 145, 146, 171
Ironsides, Mr, 92
Irving, Henry, 29
I Zingari (England), 128
I Zingari (Sydney), 55

Jackson, A. A., 109
Jackson, J., 136
Jackson, Sir Stanley, 38, 68, 73, 80, 82, 112
James, Mr, 155
Jardine, D. R., 86, 107, 111
Jeanes, W. H., 111
Jennings, J., 101
Jessop, G. L., 79, 82
Johannesburg, 84, 133
Johnston, O. A. Y., 159, 160, 164
Jones, E., 62, 73, 80, 84f
Jones, S. P., 59

Kelleway, C., 92, 171
Kelly, J. J., 37, 55, 58, 117, 159
Kelly, Mrs J. J., 58
Kelly, Ned, 42
Kent C.C.C., 35, 73, 127, 132, 135
Kermode, A., 78
Killick, E. H., 73
Kippax, A. F., 37, 105, 106, 109, 137, 167
Kipling, Rudyard, 22

Lancashire C.C.C., 68, 72, 78, 79, 133
Lane Cove C.C., 93
Lane, G., 133
Larwood, H., 86, 87, 107, 108, 110, 111, 133
Lascelles Hall, 130
Laver, F., 70, 123, 142, 143, 144
Lawry, W. M., 44, 149
Leichhardt C.C., 64
Leyton, 68, 75
Lillee, D. K., 42, 44, 104, 111
Lilley, A. A., 80, 81, 115, 118, 119, 124
Lindwall, R. R., 111
Liverpool (Aigburth), 78
Llewellyn, G. C. B., 139, 141
Lloyd, C. H., 150, 151
Lockwood, W. H., 33, 55, 64, 70, 71, 80
Lohmann, G. A., 134
'Long Stop' (*see* Hammersley, W. J.)
Lord, Thomas, 168
Lord's Cricket Ground, 35, 37, 38, 59, 67f, 82, 87, 103, 114, 126, 130, 132,

Lord's Cricket Ground [*contd.*]
168, 169
Lord's Memorial Gallery, 168
Love, H. S. B., 169
Luck, W. H., 132
'Lumpy' (*see* Stevens, E.)
Lyttelton, Hon. and Rev. E., 132
Lyttelton, Hon. R. H., 135

Macartney, C. G., 32, 33, 58, 77, 78, 109, 111, 138, 139, 142, 145, 153, 154, 171
Mackay, C., 147
MacLaren, A. C., 21, 33, 79f, 113, 132
Mailey, A. A., 26f, 160
Maley, Mr, 151
Mallett, G., 109
Manchester, 25, 115
Mandle, W. F., 126f, 136, 137
Martian, 160
Martin, F., 70
Marylebone Cricket Club, 25, 34, 35, 68, 75, 113, 131, 136, 143
Mascagni, Pietro, 22
Massie, H. H., 156
Mayne, E. R., 144f
McAlister, P. A., 144f
McAtamney, J., 36
McCabe, S. J., 36, 110, 111, 167
McClutchy, C., 48
McElhone, E., 38
McElhone, Mrs E., 38
McElhone, W. P., 143, 144
McGowan, J., 93
McIntyre, M., 133
McIntyre, Mr, 64
McKell, Sir W., 39, 93
McLauchlin, J., 66
McLeod, C. E., 71
Meckiff, I., 87
Melba, Dame Nellie, 29, 41
Melbourne, 33, 34, 45, 65, 66, 72, 87, 91, 94, 104, 111, 123, 124, 140f, 160
Melbourne Centenary Test Match, 111
Messenger, D., 154
Middlesex C.C.C., 35, 130
Molesworth, V., 148
Monfries, E., 61, 102
Moore Park, 56, 83
Moran, Dr H. M., 95
Morley, F., 133
Moses, H., Jnr, 154, 155
Moses, H., Snr, 59
Mount Keira, 56

Moyes, A. J., 153, 155
Murdoch, W. L., 42, 91, 116
Murray, D. L., 62, 63
Mycroft, W., 132
Mynn, A., 168

Napoleon I, 22, 29
Napoleonic Wars, 128
Natal, 84
Nawanagar, Jam Sahib of, 21f, 34, 35, 36, 62, 64, 71f, 109, 113, 114, 116
Newcastle, Duke of, 127
New South Wales, 33, 34, 40, 45, 50, 55, 57, 61f, 70, 85, 93, 94, 105, 109, 124, 138, 139, 143, 144, 153f, 171
Newtown, 55
New Zealand, 51, 73, 126, 147, 159, 160, 163
New Zealand Cricket Council, 159
Nicholas, Mrs M., 51
Noble, M. A., 18, 33, 50, 52, 55, 62f, 70, 73, 74, 83, 94f, 113f, 145, 153, 160, 167, 171
Noonan, Mr, 64
North Sydney C.C., 64
'Not Out' (*see* Davis, J. C.)
Not Test Cricket, 61
Nottinghamshire C.C.C., 32, 128, 129, 134, 136
Nourse, A. D., 140, 141

O'Connor, J. A., 171
O'Hara, J., 170
Oldfield, W. A., 36
'Old Steve', 48, 49
Old Trafford, 25, 33, 68, 73, 79, 81, 82, 113, 115, 136
On Top Down Under, 67
O'Reilly, W. J., 26, 54, 111, 152
Oscroft, W., 133
Oval, The (Kennington), 36, 68, 71, 74, 76, 82, 85, 113, 116, 131, 134
Oxford University C.C., 72, 74

Packer, Clyde, 148
Packer, Sir Frank, 148
Packer, Kerry, 147f
Packer, R. C., 147, 148
Paddington, 18, 19, 27, 29, 47f, 63, 64, 66, 87, 90f, 109, 167, 170
Pakistan, 150
Palairet, L. C. H., 79
Palairet, R. C. N., 108

Pardon, S. H., 79
Parr, G., 137
Pearse, O. C., 140
Peel, R., 55, 64, 135
Perth, 90, 104, 108, 125
Phar Lap, 42
Philadelphia, 133
Pickwick Papers, The, 128
Pilch, Fuller, 128
Pitt, William, the Younger, 22
Ponsford, W. H., 77
Port Adelaide, 86
Pretoria, 83, 84
Pring, Mr Justice, 155, 156
Professional Cricketer in England in the Nineteenth Century, The 127

Quarterly Review, 43
Queensland, 62, 73, 143, 144

Radcliffe-on-Trent, 129
Ramadhin, S., 139
Ranjitsinhji, K. S. (*see* Nawanagar, Jam Sahib of)
Ransford, V. S., 139f, 153, 160, 161, 167
Raphael, F. C., 159
Redfern C.C., 27, 64, 83, 91f
Reese, D., 17, 160
Relf, A. E., 114f
Referee (New Zealand), 160
Referee (Sydney), 56, 87, 90, 91, 115
Rhodes, Sir H., 160
Rhodes, W., 33, 36, 74, 80, 81, 82, 114f, 121, 122, 123, 136, 137, 168
Richards, B. A., 152
Richards, I. V. A., 152
Richardson, T., 55, 62, 111, 134
Richardson, V. Y., 107, 126
Richmond, Duke of, 127
Robey, George, 78
Robinson, Ray, 67
Rogerson, S., 136, 137
Root, F., 137
Rose, T., 18
Rosenwater, Irving, 38
Rush, H., 144
Ryan, 'Paddy', 63
Ryder, J., 153, 154

Sandham, A., 36
Sandwich, Earl of, 127
Saunders, J. C., 159
Saunders, J. V., 34, 79, 80, 81, 83, 94, 114, 116, 123
Schwarz, R. O., 138, 139, 140
Scott, J., 111
Sewell, E. H. D., 77
Shaw, A., 85, 129, 132
Sheffield, Bramall Lane, 79, 82, 103
Sheffield, Lord, 132
Sheffield Shield, 62, 132
Sheridan, P., 167, 168
Sherwell, P. W., 139, 140, 141
Sims, Sir A., 147, 160, 161
Sinclair, K., 168
Smith, Mrs G., 51
Smith, Sir J., 147, 148
Smith, Sidney, Jnr, 40, 144, 146
Smith, Admiral Sir V. A. T., 51
Smith's Weekly, 147
Snooke, S. J., 141
Snow, J. A., 111
Sobers, Sir G. St A., 34
Somerset C.C.C., 72
South Africa, 22, 38, 69, 83, 84, 111, 127, 129, 133, 138f, 151, 168
South Australia, 55, 57, 61, 65, 84f, 122, 143, 144
South Sydney C.C., 56f, 93
South Sydney R.F.C., 52
Southland, 160
Spiers and Pond, 45
Spofforth, F. R., 42
Spooner, R. H., 21
Sporting Magazine, 59, 60
Stackpole, K. R., 111, 149
Star, 84
Stephenson, H. H., 134
Stevens, E., 128
Stoddart, A. E., 54, 62f
Street, Sir K., 154
Street, Sir L., 154
Street, Sir P., 154
Strudwick, H., 38, 111, 112
Sullivan, J., 41
Sun-News Pictorial, 75
Surrey C.C.C., 35, 68, 72, 127, 131, 134
Surrey Hills, 58
Sussex C.C.C., 34, 35, 69f, 127, 132
Sutcliffe, H., 33, 36
Sutton (Notts), 129
Sydney, 18, 19, 25f, 45f, 62f, 78, 84f, 101, 110f, 124, 125, 137f, 167, 170
Sydney Morning Herald, 67f
Sydney Sun, 108
Sydney Telegraph, 138, 140, 157

Tankerville, Lord, 127, 128
Tantanoola, 55
Tasmania, 73, 144
Tate, F. W., 79, 81, 82
Tate, M. W., 77, 79, 81, 92
Taunton, 72
10 for 66 and All That, 26
Test Tussles on and off the Field, 66, 142
33 Years of Cricket, 18
Thomson, J. R., 44, 62, 63, 111, 125, 126, 151
Times, The, 69
Town and Country Journal, 58
Transvaal, 83
Trent Bridge, 32, 38, 68, 78, 151
Trevor, Colonel Philip, 21, 22, 23, 44
Triangular Tournament, 142
Trott, A. E., 85
Trott, G. H. S., 84, 85
Trueman, F. S., 149
Trumble, H., 65, 66, 71, 75, 80f, 124
Trumper, Alice (sister), 51
Trumper, Ann Louise (daughter), 58, 166, 167
Trumper, Charles (father), 51f, 167, 171
Trumper, Mrs Charles (née Louise Coughlan) (mother), 51, 58, 64, 167
Trumper, Charles Ernest (brother), 37, 51, 57, 171
Trumper, F., 60
Trumper, May (sister) (*see* Nicholas, Mrs M.)
Trumper, Sidney (brother), 51, 57, 171
Trumper, Mrs Sidney (sister-in-law), 59
Trumper, Una (sister) (*see* Smith, Mrs G.)
Trumper, Mrs Victor (née Sarah Ann Briggs) (wife), 25, 37, 40, 57, 58, 158, 165f
Trumper, Victor, Jnr (son), 58, 158, 166, 167
Trumper Park, 18, 49, 50, 90, 167
Trumper Testimonial Fund, Victor, 154f
Truro, 71
Turner, C. T. B., 85, 156, 171

Tyldesley, J. T., 79, 123

Verity, H., 111
Victoria, 34, 45, 61, 65, 66, 85, 86, 102, 117, 143, 144, 154
Voce, W., 107, 111

Waddy, Rev. E. F., 138, 160
Walker, I. D., 168
Walker, M. H. N., 62
Wardill, Major B. J., 66
Warner, Sir P. F., 103, 107, 108, 113, 118, 120f, 154
Warwick (NSW), 56, 58
Warwickshire C.C.C., 72
Was it all Cricket?, 17
Waverley, 26, 51, 63, 64, 105, 111, 137, 154, 171
West Indies, 79, 90, 125, 150, 151
Whitty, Mrs M., 55
Whitty, W. J., 55, 57, 153
Wilde, Oscar, 38
Willett, Miss M., 168
Williams, E., 154, 155
Winchelsea, Earl of, 127
Winning, C. S., 18
Winter, G. E., 70
Wisden, 79, 145
Wisden, J., 168
Wolfes Schnappes, 155
Wood, J., 167, 168
Woodfull, W. M., 107, 108
Woods, S. M. J., 168
Woollahra, 51
Woolley, F. E., 168
Worcester, 68
World of Cricket, The (Ed. Swanton), 40

'Yabba' (*see* Gascoigne, Mr)
Yorkshire C.C.C., 72, 78, 122, 135, 136, 151
Young, H., 68

Zulch, J. W., 141

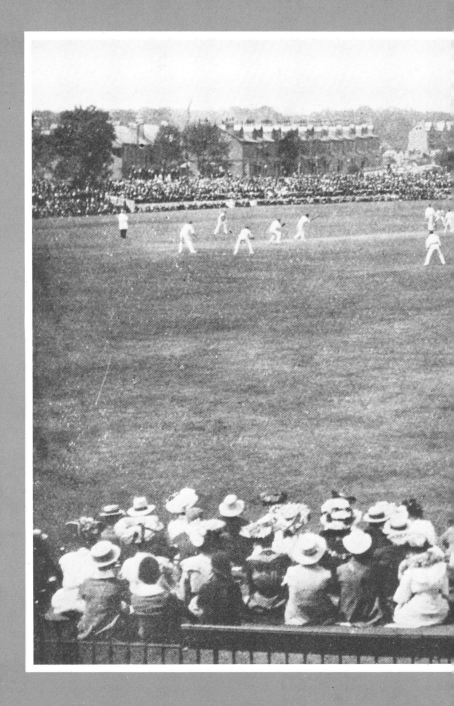